THE
SIMPLE TRUTH

THE
SIMPLE TRUTH

FORTY-TWO
PERSONAL ENCOUNTERS

Joseph Schmidt

ISBN: 979-8-6837-2088-9

DEDICATION

To my sons, Justin and Jeremy. This book was written for them.

ACKNOWLEDGMENTS

With deep gratitude to my editor, Felicia Halpert; to Tom Wise and Jay Friedman for their advice; and to my wife, Kathryn, for bearing with me.

Cover photo by Joseph Schmidt:
Land's End, southernmost point in India.

We're all just finding our way back home.

CONTENTS

The names have not been changed to protect the guilty.

OMAHA

KINDERGARTEN

I **WAS** afraid it would happen, and it did. I'm sitting at my kindergarten desk, waiving my hand in the air. Our teacher, Mrs. Shell, had instructed us to raise our hands if we wanted to either speak or have a bathroom break.

I rarely spoke, but I did need a break.

When I started kindergarten at Cross Lutheran School in Omaha, Nebraska I liked having my desk in the back of the room. I could hide and not be seen. Now, as I waived my hand, I saw how this might become a problem.

Someone in the front of the room was speaking so I had to wait my turn. After that speaker finished, another classmate flung up her hand. Mrs. Shell called on her and I had to wait again. The girl, Viola, spoke for a long time, and I was beginning to feel desperate. Viola sat on the opposite side of the classroom and Ms. Shell was only looking in her direction.

When Viola finally finished, I shot my hand back up, but Mrs. Shell wasn't looking around anymore.

Instead, she told us to finish another lesson in our workbook. Then she returned to her desk and began working on her lesson plans. That's when I became frantic and began to waive my arm back and forth.

Mrs. Shell was firm with her rules. I'd witnessed several other classmates receive stern reprimands for speaking or moving from their desks without permission. I was intent on obeying the rules.

Then it happened. I looked down and saw a small wet spot on my pants.

Something had to be done. Sitting in the back row, I knew there was a storage closet just behind my desk. Looking back, I noticed the closet door was slightly open, offering a clear invitation. Quietly, I stood up and slipped into the closet. The rest of the class was focused on their workbooks and didn't notice. Mrs. Shell was busy with lesson plans and didn't notice either.

The closet was stocked with arts, crafts, and janitorial supplies. Then I saw what I needed: a large janitorial bucket standing in the back corner. My sense of desperation was quickly resolved. The next step was to return to my desk.

With the door slightly cracked open, I peered into the classroom, and my anxiety returned. Mrs. Shell was standing in front of the room and talking to the class again. Not wanting to be seen, I remained hidden in the closet, waiting for a chance to sneak back to my desk.

That chance never came.

I was still in the closet when class was over for the day. Mrs. Shell dismissed the students and they filed out.

No one noted my absence. Once the children were gone, Mrs. Shell returned to her desk and continued working on her lesson plans. Not wanting to be found out, I stayed silent, quietly remaining in the closet.

After about ten minutes, Mrs. Shell was ready to leave. She briefly walked around the room straightening things up for the next day. As she walked by the closet, my teacher firmly pushed the door shut and turned the latch.

I was locked in.

I should have said something at that point, but I just stood in the dark as she finished up and left for home. I did not have a good feeling about things. There was no window or light in the closet. I just stood there, waiting.

After fifteen minutes or so, the janitor came into the classroom and opened the closet to get his supplies. Even after he opened the door and peered inside, I remained quiet, knowing I had broken the rules. The janitor was startled when he saw me standing there. But neither of us said anything. The janitor didn't want to break any rules either. So, he focused on getting his mop and pail, while I slipped by him and out into the open.

The next day in class, the first thing I did was to raise my hand. When Ms. Shell gave me permission to speak, I was ready. I asked if she could move my desk to the front of the room.

I wanted to be seen.

BENITA

JERRY had a score to settle with our sister, Benita. Given that Jerry was my big brother, and I was only nine at the time, I agreed to be the active agent in his plan. It was payback time.

Our house was a spacious pre-war home on the outskirts of Omaha with three bedrooms on the second floor and a master bedroom on the main floor. It was surrounded by wide lawns and tall, dark, oak trees. When the wind blew, the tree branches would move and scratch against the upstairs windowpanes. In the late evening hours, this scratching sound was particularly creepy.

Benita was twelve years old and the oldest child in the family. Her bedroom was on the second floor at the back end of the house. There were several tall oak trees just outside of her bedroom window. Jerry and I shared a bedroom a few paces down the hall, not far from the stairway to the main floor. My parents had the master bedroom downstairs.

On the chosen night, Jerry and I put on our flannel pajamas, closed the door, and waited in our room.

A few minutes later, when Benita left her room to brush her teeth, Jerry smiled and nodded at me. It was time to activate his plan. While Jerry remained in our room, I slipped quietly out, and tip-toed down the hall into Benita's room. Once there, I bent down and slid under her bed. Lying on the cool hard wood floor in my flannel pajamas, I waited silently in the dark.

When Benita finished brushing her teeth, I could hear her footsteps coming down the hall and enter her bedroom. I peeked out from beneath the bed and saw Benita's feet and ankles walking up to the bed. When she climbed in, the mattress above me sagged and almost touched my face. Benita squirmed above me for a few moments, found a comfortable position, and settled in for the night. I remained quiet, holding my breath.

I waited until she was completely still. Then I heard an oak branch brush against her window. That was my cue: I made a quick scratching sound with my fingernails on the bottom of her mattress. I sensed Benita's body stiffen. But my scratching had been faint, and she may have thought it was just her imagination.

I waited quietly again until her body began to soften and relax. The oak branch scraped against the window again and I immediately followed with my own scratching sound on the bottom of the mattress. This time I scratched more loudly and got Benita's attention. Her body froze in a rigid position under the blankets above me. Then I stopped. She was totally still.

A few seconds later I suddenly began scratching very loudly. Adding to the effect, I grabbed the mattress above me with both hands and began to shake it. Benita had heard enough. Her body sprang to life and she quickly swung her legs over the side of the bed. From my position below, I saw her foot and ankle land on the floor about two feet from my face.

This was the moment Jerry was waiting for. Making a deep guttural sound, I shot out both hands from under the bed and grabbed Benita by the right ankle. That's when the shrieking began. Without looking down to see what had attached itself to her ankle, Benita exploded across the room, running for the door. I hung onto her ankle with both hands as she ran, sliding on my stomach, face-first, along the hard wood floor.

With high decibel shrieks she picked up speed, dashing through her bedroom doorway and down the hall. I didn't let go and was dragged along at floor level. Familiar surroundings flew by me at a rapid rate. We careened past my bedroom and continued on to the top of the stairs. Finally, I released her ankle; the ride was over. Benita continued to shriek as she flew down the stairs and ran to our parents' bedroom.

Still lying on the floor, I looked back towards the bedroom I shared with Jerry. The door was cracked slightly open and I saw Jerry's grinning face peeking out. Benita and Jerry would have more battles, but the score was settled for now.

FROGGY

HIS given name was David, but we called him Froggy. You could see the resemblance in his facial features, particularly in his large, unceasing smile.

Unfortunately, Froggy did not brush his teeth and his smile was not that attractive. His front teeth were green, mossy, and prominent, with large gaps separating them. It didn't help that his smile was so persistent.

Froggy was probably seven or eight, a couple of years younger than the group of boys I hung out with at church. But he insisted on following us around and getting in the way. He could be very annoying. To his credit though, Froggy was tough and relentless as a badger. My group was made up of an immature and insensitive bunch of kids, but Froggy seemed impervious to our taunts. He persisted in pursuing us, seemed to thrive on his outsider status, and gleefully participated in our attempts to keep him away.

Things with Froggy came to a head at the Sunday School pancake eating contest. All the Sunday school

9

kids loved pancakes, and everyone entered the contest. There was no downside. Win or lose, we could eat all the pancakes we wanted. As a Mennonite, I knew the value of a healthy appetite. And with my taste for pancakes, I liked my chances in the contest.

On the day of the contest, the church basement hummed with activity. Several women were happily working at the stove, flipping pancakes, and stacking them high onto platters. Dishes of butter and pitchers of maple syrup were placed on several long tables. The kids eagerly waited to dig in. After a blessing from the minister, we all sat down in rows and the contest began.

Everyone got one pancake at a time, finished it, and then asked for another. There was a server assigned to each row of kids to keep count. Things started fast. Everyone loved pancakes. Even the younger kids were digging in, some making it to six or seven servings before dropping out.

After thirteen or fourteen pancakes, some of the boys in my group of friends were too stuffed to continue and slunk away. At seventeen pancakes, most contestants had dropped out.

By the time we hit twenty, we were down to three kids: a big teenager, Froggy, and me.

Froggy was sitting next to me. His routine was simple and straightforward. He ate each pancake quickly with lots of syrup and butter. Each time he finished a pancake he put down his fork, smiled broadly, and boldly stated, "Bring me another!"

The big teenager dropped out at number twenty-two. He was embarrassed to have been bested by Froggy and slunk away like the others. Now it was just the two of us: Froggy and me.

I tried to look confident, finishing each pancake and requesting another, but I was getting worried. I was feeling extremely bloated and began experiencing a strange sense of heaviness. This heaviness extended outwards from my stomach and seemed to fill the entire room. Meanwhile, there was Froggy, with his bold and relentless, "Bring me another!" And each time he finished another pancake, there was that mossy, toothy grin.

When we reached number twenty-five, I was ready to bail out and crawl away. But to avoid humiliation, I managed to force the pancake down. A heavy dose of syrup and butter helped. That's when the contest ended.

We both had just finished our twenty-fifth pancake. Froggy, true to form, smiled broadly and opened his mouth to demand another. But as he tried to speak, I noticed Froggy's teeth were tightly clenched. Instead of hearing words, I saw pancake puree oozing slowly out through the gaps between his front teeth. It was not a pretty sight. He was completely backed up.

Putting my own sense of discomfort aside, I quietly asked for one more. When it was served, I took one small bite, put down my fork, and pushed the plate away. It was over.

Looking at Froggy sitting next to me, I felt a new respect. There he sat, half my size, teeth clenched, oozing pancakes. He was utterly resilient, that persistent smile still radiating from his face.

MR. LINK

OTTO K. Link was the principle at Cross Lutheran Elementary School in Omaha. Nobody crossed him. He ruled the school with an iron fist and an intimidating glare. With his steel gray crew-cut, hard muscular physique, and volatile temper, he was not to be messed with. Some of the older boys referred to him as the "Missing Link," but this was always done behind his back and spoken in a whisper.

Mr. Link served as school principal, and he also taught sixth, seventh, and eighth grades — all in one classroom. He would give out assignments for one grade to work on while he taught a lesson to another grade. Mr. Link kept all three grades busy, teaching them in rotation. Everything was well organized. No one spoke or left their desk until the bell rang for recess, for lunch, or when school was out.

He did give us occasional breaks, though. From time to time Mr. Link would leave us with our assignments and walk to his office across the hall. While he worked in the office, things would loosen up in the classroom.

Things were going well for me during the first few months of sixth grade. I was quiet, diligent, and completed my assignments. I aimed to please and was a model student. I'd heard frightening stories about what had happened to students who had crossed Mr. Link, and that was not going to be me.

During this time, I had also developed an infatuation with Lorraine, a classmate who sat at her desk two rows to my right. I thought she might have feelings for me too, but it was hard to tell for sure. Our relationship didn't involve much talking, just side-long glances, and awkward smiles. I was determined to take things up a notch. I just needed the right opportunity to make my move.

One afternoon, Mr. Link gave us our assignments and left the classroom for his office. The class remained quiet as we did our work. Upon finishing, I looked over to my right where Lorraine was sitting. She had finished her work too. This could be my opportunity. A smile from her would make my day.

So, I took out a sheet of paper, and wrote a short note saying that I really liked her and hoped she liked me too. Having written the note, my confidence was rising, and I decided to follow through. Folding the note into a small packet, I aimed it in her direction and lobbed it through the air. The note bounced off Lorraine's desk and landed on the floor. At that same moment, I heard the classroom door open behind me. Mr. Link had returned. I knew that the classroom door had windows at eye level, so he must have seen everything. A deep hush fell over the room.

The old hardwood floor creaked as Mr. Link slowly walked up behind me. I could feel him glaring at the back of my head. There was a sensation of heat surging from my stomach and up through my chest. The back of my neck felt hot and prickly. I could hear him breathing heavily as he stood not more than a foot behind my desk.

My heart was pounding in anticipation; I wasn't sure what he would do. Then I felt Mr. Link grip my left ear tight between his thumb and forefinger. I continued facing forward, trying to comprehend my situation. Keeping his grip on my ear, he began to pull it upwards. The force of his grip was increasing, and I began to hear crackling sounds. The cartilage in my ear was giving way. I did not resist as he pulled me up, out of my chair. He marched me, by the ear, to the front of the room. Then, to show he meant business, Mr. Link pulled me up to the blackboard and flattened my nose against the hard, chalky surface. After one final squeeze, he released my ear and slowly walked to his desk. No words had been spoken.

I stood there with my nose jammed against the blackboard. My ear was burning. I knew Lorraine was looking at me from behind. I wondered if she had read the note. I hoped not.

LESTER

I **WAS** in a rush. Junior high football practice started in an hour and I had to finish mowing the lawn before going. It was a big lawn, and the mower was big too. The mower had a loud, powerful engine and was self-driven with a hand clutch. Push the clutch handle forward, and the mower moved forward. Pull it back, and the mower stopped.

Not wanting to be late for practice, I ratcheted up the speed and trotted behind the mower. I had mastered my mowing technique and quickly maneuvered the heavy mower around trees and bushes that stood in our path. I wore my white sneakers and moved nimbly along, careening around the yard at a fast pace. The job was moving along well, and I was confident about finishing in time for practice.

As I was approaching my last turn, I pushed the mower around the corner and released the clutch. I was in a rush and must have been careless. My left foot slipped forward on the wet grass. In an instant it was under the mower and into the path of the whirling mower blade. I heard a sickening "thwack" as the blade hit my foot. I didn't feel any pain, just a deep heaviness moving up my left leg. I quickly yanked my foot out from under the mower and fearfully looked down to assess the damage. The first thing I noticed was that my white sneaker was quickly turning red. I also saw that the front part of the shoe was lopped off, but I couldn't see my toes. Suddenly everything around me took on a surreal tone. The air seemed thick and steamy. I heard a strange roaring noise in my ears.

No one was at home, so I began hopping on my good foot. My goal was to make it to my friend Lester's house across the street.

Lester was two years older than me and a very unusual character. He greased his hair straight back with motor oil, knew hundreds of off-color jokes, and was always in trouble with his parents. He passed the time roaring up and down our street in his hot Ford coupe. Lester was always full of enthusiasm. He just lacked focus.

Lester was washing his coupe when I hopped across the street and into his driveway. He immediately saw my bloody sneaker and moved into action. This was a medical emergency and he was thrilled at the opportunity to be the "first responder." Lester quickly fired up his car and helped me into the front seat. With a staccato beat blasting from his tail pipes, he pushed the gas pedal to the floor and sped full throttle toward town. Along the way, Lester squeezed out every ounce of acceleration the Ford could offer, shifting up and down through his manual 4-speed transmission at every opportunity.

Lester delivered without a hitch. The doctor took me in, cut off my mangled sneaker, and evaluated the damage to my foot. He gave a soft whistle and told me I was lucky: I'd only lost the end of my big toe. My foot was badly bruised, but there was no other serious damage. After finding the end of my toe lodged inside my sneaker, he sewed it back on and wrapped my foot in thick bandages. That was it. I could go.

Lester was waiting in his car, revving the engine, and listening to the popping staccato of his tail pipes. To be prepared, he had kept the car running. He was serious about completing the second half of his mission. He helped me into the passenger seat, then climbed behind the steering wheel and hit the throttle. With tires spinning, we shot away. Every second counted.

Lester got me to football practice on time. Naturally, the coach took one look at my foot and told us to go home. Again, Lester was ready. He jumped behind the wheel, fired up his Ford, and we sped away. I was home within minutes.

Lester had found a new sense of purpose that day. He was focused and he delivered.

HOOPS OOPS

I WAS beginning to make a name for myself on the ninth-grade basketball team in junior high. I had just finished the football season when the basketball coach, Mr. Mitchell, asked me to try out for the team. I knew I could rebound well and was soon jumping high enough to dunk. My shooting skills were rather erratic, but I had also developed a reputation for remaining calm in high pressure situations. At least that's what Coach Mitchell thought.

After a week or two of practice, the coach put me on the first team in the center position. It wasn't long before I began making a positive impact. I led the league in rebounds and was starting to develop a decent hook shot. One of our guards was a great shooter and we also had the best ninth-grade offensive forward in the county. So, the team did not need me to score that much. I just had to be calm and steady. Coach Mitchell could not abide a player who got too excited. He liked players with poise, players who would not choke.

Our team was talented, and we soon found our natural rhythm, steadily improving during the early season. By Christmas break we were on a roll. That's when we were scheduled to play South Omaha, the highpoint of our basketball season. The game would be highly competitive and the fan base for each team – students, parents, friends, and alumni – was fiercely loyal, and adamant about winning. Coach Mitchell, for all his emphasis on having a calm and steady demeanor, was actually quite an excitable character. As we approached the game with South Omaha, he began to express his emotions more freely.

The big game was to be held on a Saturday evening and everyone was jacked-up with anticipation. Coach Mitchell could not contain himself, making a flurry of phone calls to each team member before the game, urging us to remain calm and steady and warning us not to choke.

That evening the South Omaha team, a perpetual basketball powerhouse, burst confidently out of their locker room and onto the court in bright red uniforms. Our team, not quite as confident, was decked out in blue and gold. The fans for both teams stood and cheered, elevating adrenaline levels all around. As we ran warm-up drills, Coach Mitchell could not sit still for more than a few seconds. He jumped up repeatedly and ran onto the court, waving his arms and shouting out instructions.

The referee blew his whistle and the game started. Surprisingly, our team jumped out to an early lead. Our shooting guard and forward were hot and I was rebounding well. We had our adrenalin level under control and were in the flow as a team. At halftime, we led by seven points.

Things changed for us in the second half. South Omaha had an all-star guard who could rain long-range bombs into the bucket. He had not been a factor in the first half, but the second half was different. He began to hit his shots and our lead slipped. It was soon a tie game. A short time later we were five points down.

With about five minutes remaining, we clawed our way back. The game seesawed back and forth, each team taking the lead briefly and then losing it. With about eight seconds to go, we scored again and were up by one point. South Omaha immediately called a timeout and both teams gathered around their coaches.

Coach Mitchell's eyes were bulging out. His arms waved wildly, and he shouted incoherently. It didn't really matter what he was saying. We all knew what was happening next. The South Omaha all-star would get the ball and go for the final shot. If he made it, the game was over. If he missed, then I had to get the rebound and we would win. When the timeout ended, Coach Mitchell was yelling louder than ever, "Stay calm! Don't choke!"

The last few seconds of the game began according to script. South Omaha's all-star quickly dribbled down the court and picked up a screen at the top of the key. He made a jab-step toward the bucket to shake his defender and then rose to shoot. As he released the ball, I positioned myself to rebound, sliding into the lane. The ball was slightly long and hit the back of the rim. I shifted my weight and jumped as high as I could. My timing was perfect. I soared over the rim and cleanly collected the ball with both hands. This was my rebound. The game was ours.

In this same moment, though, I felt a subtle and irrational urge. My hands were right over the hoop and holding the ball. I was looking at the easiest shot of my life. Calmly and steadily, but completely unexpectedly, I dropped the ball into their hoop. The gym fell quiet. I'd shot the ball in the wrong basket and scored two points for South Omaha.

Game over. We had lost by one point.

I looked over at Coach Mitchell. His arms were raised in the air and, though his mouth was wide open, he was no longer shouting. After a moment, he dropped his arms and slumped down on the bench. He sat there quietly, looking down at his hands. I slowly walked over to the bench and sat down next to him. With my head hanging down I studied my sneakers. He continued to study his hands.

We were both calm. But not very steady.

DAD

TOOLBOX

I T WAS a summer evening in Omaha and Dad was doing plumbing repairs in the basement. My mom was in the kitchen as usual, cooking and cleaning. I was hanging out on the front porch with nothing to do. Then my dad called out from below. He wanted his toolbox.

I sprang into action and ran to the tool closet. Given that I was only six years old, the toolbox was big and heavy. Using both hands, I was able to lift it from the shelf. I could handle this. I carried the box to the top of the stairs and began my descent to the basement.

Holding the toolbox steady, I took slow steps down the stairs, one at a time. About halfway, I could feel my arms beginning to weaken. But I tightened my grip and continued downwards, step by step.

When my hands began to shake, I knew I didn't have much time. I had to move more quickly.

That was a mistake.

I lost my balance. Then I lost my grip. The box tumbled down the stairs. It picked up speed, and then finally crashed onto the basement floor. Tools scattered in every direction. I followed right behind, tumbling head over heels and landing in a heap at the bottom.

I lay on the floor, my stomach pressed against the cold, hard cement. Wrenches, screwdrivers, nails, and bolts were scattered all around me.

Then, I turned my head. Out of the corner of my eye, I saw Dad. He was grabbing a long, thin length of wood and moving towards me. There was fire in his eyes.

"Don't just lie there with your teeth in your mouth," he growled, towering over me. Pick up your mess!" Then he swung the long piece of wood and hit me with a stinging blow on the back of my thighs.

He only hit me once. But he made his point.

I stood up stiffly. The raw exposed walls, and low unfinished ceiling, made the basement feel grim and claustrophobic. I slowly picked up the tools, carefully placing them back in the toolbox.

When I was finished, I left the toolbox on the floor, walked back upstairs, and began to cry.

'55 CHEVY

I HAD just turned eight when my dad bought a new 1955 Chevy. It was a two-tone, blue and white sedan, and the first year Chevy offered a V8 engine. With 265 cubic inches under the hood, it was quite a hot car.

My dad was known to have a lead foot, so having a more powerful car was exactly what he wanted. Jerry and I were excited when Dad took the family out for our first ride. It was Sunday evening, and we had a church service to attend.

Dad had a smile on his face and a gleam in his eye as he gunned the Chevy. We easily sped past cars he would have previously followed. We pulled up in front of our church with a flourish, parked, and entered the sanctuary. Dad was an ordained Mennonite minister, and he gave the sermon that night, holding the congregation's rapt attention. He spoke about Sampson and Delilah, my favorite bible story.

After the service, I hurried outside and met my friends in front of the church. I proudly showed them our new Chevy, pointing out the V8 insignia and the whitewall tires. Everyone was impressed.

On the drive home, my dad stopped at Zesto's and bought the family ice cream cones. The new Chevy looked great in the parking lot and several customers walked over to check it out. We all enjoyed the attention.

Once we arrived home, Dad carefully pulled the Chevy into the garage and we all piled out. I was the last to leave the car, and I turned to slam the door shut. My little brother, Jimmy, was already out of the car, but his hand was still resting in the door frame.

The door slammed on his fingers. When Jimmy screamed, I realized what I'd done. I yanked the door back open and pulled out his hand. A wave of nausea surged through me because of what I had done.

My dad came over from the other side of the car and looked closely at Jimmy's hand. The fingers were bruised and bleeding, but there were no broken bones.

Then Dad gave me a look I had come to dread. "See what you've done!" he snapped. "I'll show you what it feels like!"

With that, he opened the car door and told me to put my hand in the door frame, right where Jimmy's hand had been.

Slowly, I put my hand in the door. I noticed it was shaking. My dad paused a few seconds, then suddenly grabbed the car door, and began to swing it shut. A moment before the door could crush my hand, he pulled the door back and walked away.

I pulled my hand back from the door and held it close to my chest. Another wave of nausea surged through me. This time it was for what my dad had done.

FISHING

MY DAD liked to fish. He'd wear his lucky yellow hat and use his favorite fishing rod. Dad was a practical man and having one rod was enough for him. When he took my brother and me out fishing, one rod would have to do.

We were on a family vacation at Blue Lake in Minnesota when I first had an opportunity to try my dad's fishing rod. Soon after we arrived, Dad, my brother Jerry, and I jumped in a rowboat and headed out onto the lake. The fishing here was supposed to be good and we were all excited. Jerry and I were especially hopeful about the possibility of catching our first fish. I was about eight years old at the time and going fishing in a boat was a new adventure for me.

We stopped rowing about fifty yards from the shore. Dad baited the hook with corn meal paste and added a lead sinker for extra weight. Then, pressing on the fishing line with his thumb, he cocked his arm back and whipped the rod forward.

The bait and sinker hurtled through the air and plunked into the water a good distance from the boat.

Dad slowly reeled the line back in, hoping for a bite. Nothing. He continued to cast out the line, and then reel it back in. But no bites; no fish.

Since he wasn't having any luck, my dad eventually handed the rod to Jerry. Jerry didn't have any luck either. When it was my turn, I imagined how neat it would be if I brought in the first fish. I could earn some respect.

As I gripped the smooth cork handle of the fishing rod, my excitement rose. The weight of the rod felt good in my hand. Dad pointed to a shady spot far from the boat and asked if I could cast that far. He was pointing out what he thought was the best spot to catch a fish.

My confidence ebbed a bit. The shady spot was a long way off. But I didn't want to disappoint my dad and was determined to do my best. So, I cocked my arm back and whipped the rod forward with all my strength. To get extra distance, I snapped my wrist sharply forward at the end of my throwing motion.

I immediately felt two unexpected sensations. The first came through my sense of touch. The cork handle was more slippery than I anticipated. The sensation I felt in my fingers was one of loss. What had been in my hand was no longer there.

The second sensation was visual. My eyes followed the long high trajectory of the fishing rod – as well as the bait, hook, line, and sinker – as it flew through the air. The flight of the fishing rod was a beautiful thing to see while it lasted. But then the rod splashed down into Blue Lake, almost reaching the spot I had aimed for.

As we watched from the boat, the rod started to sink. Before my dad could say anything, I jumped out of the boat and swam furiously toward the shady spot. When I arrived, the fishing rod had disappeared.

Looking back at the boat, I saw my dad sitting there in his lucky yellow hat. There was a dark expression on his face. Then I looked toward the shore which was clearly further away than the boat. My decision was made. I swam for shore.

DRIVE-IN

DRINKING, smoking, dancing, and going to movies were strictly forbidden in our Mennonite community. My dad, being a Mennonite minister, was inflexible in these matters. So of course, when the opportunity presented itself, I jumped at the chance to see my first movie.

As usual, my older brother Jerry was involved in leading me astray. He told me that a small group of his friends was planning a trip to a drive-in movie theater. At ten years old, I was younger than the others, but I was eager to join them if invited.

On the way to the drive-in it became clear that there was not enough money to buy tickets for everyone. Two of us would need to sneak in. Being the youngest, Jerry and I were selected for that role. I was not enthusiastic about this. But when the car stopped a few blocks from the drive-in, Jerry and I got out of the car and crawled into the trunk.

When the trunk was closed it was darker than I expected. The pungent odor from the exhaust was not pleasant either. Jerry and I felt cut off from his friends. We could hear them talking and laughing as they sat a few feet away inside the car.

Jerry and I lay quietly in the trunk as the car stopped at the drive-in entrance and the guys in the car paid for their tickets. They then drove to an open parking spot, stopped the car, and hooked a small movie speaker onto the car window. Jerry and I had been lying in the trunk for some time now. So, it was a relief to hear one of the guys finally get out of the car, walk back to the trunk, and slide the car key into the lock.

After being trapped in the stuffy trunk, the evening air felt cool and refreshing. I quickly scrambled out and jumped into the back seat of the car. I was excited. This was my first movie.

A few minutes later, two stern men came up to our car and asked to see everyone's tickets. Hearing this request, my excitement began to diminish. Jerry and I didn't have tickets. We were caught. The drive-in security guards had spotted us crawling out of the trunk. The guards had seen this trick before and knew what to look for.

After Jerry and I confessed, the guards walked us over to the manager's office. To my surprise, the manager was not too hard on us. After lecturing us briefly, it seemed like he was about to let us go. I began to breathe more easily.

Then came the shocker. The manager said he was going to call our parents. He was going to tell Mom and Dad what happened.

This was not good.

The manager took our home phone number and sent us back to the car. I had no interest in watching the movie after that.

When it was over, the drive home felt painfully slow. Jerry and I dreaded the prospect of facing Dad. His punishments were typically painful, sometimes in the form of a shoe or belt being laid briskly on our backsides.

When we arrived home, Dad was waiting. But there was no lecture, no shoe, no belt. He just had a curious look in his eye when he asked, "How was the movie? I've never seen one."

OKLAHOMA

UNCLE HANK

WORKING on Uncle Hank's wheat farm in Oklahoma taught me a lot of things, such as working hard and taking responsibility. It also taught me how to earn a few dollars by using my hands.

I was eleven years old, my first summer on the farm, and a "dollar a day" wage sounded like a good deal. Hank was my mom's brother and we all agreed that I was ready for some real work. Most of my work time was spent alone, plowing the fields on Uncle Hank's M&M tractor, or driving his wheat truck from the field to the storage elevators. The early summer days in Oklahoma were hot, dry, and peaceful. Golden wheat fields flowed to the horizon in all directions.

Uncle Hank would occasionally vary the work routine and ask me to help him with a special project. These endeavors were usually a welcome change of pace. And since Hank was a man of few words, a special project provided an opportunity for my Uncle to say those few words to me.

On one project, he asked for help making repairs on his windmill. In Oklahoma, the wind never stops, and his windmill had been turning faithfully for many years, pumping out water for his cattle. But the main bolt connecting the pumping shaft to the windmill had recently sheared off deep in the well. It had to be replaced.

Hank said it would be a simple job. He'd climb down a steep iron ladder into the well and replace the bolt. I would stay on top and keep the shaft from turning so he could do his work. Uncle Hank handed me a large, heavy monkey wrench and showed me where to grip the shaft. His only advice to me was: "Don't drop it." With that, he climbed down the iron rungs deep into the well.

When he got to the bottom, Uncle Hank found the broken bolt and prepared to remove it from the shaft. "Hold on tight," he yelled, "I'm twisting it out!"

This was my first summer working on the farm, and I was motivated to please. I gripped the wrench tightly with both hands so the shaft wouldn't turn.

But then an odd thing happened. Hank was turning the shaft to the right – not to the left, as I expected. I watched in disbelief as the heavy monkey wrench moved away from me. I watched as it slipped out of my hands.

I should have called out to warn Hank, but I'd lost my voice. Only my eyes seemed to work. They were gauging the position of the wrench as it tumbled. The heavy wrench fell silently, gaining momentum rapidly as it hurtled downward.

The only good news is that Hank was leaning over the shaft and not standing up. The wrench hit him in the back of his neck and not on the head. That might have killed him.

When the wrench found its mark, Uncle Hank gasped and slumped to the ground. He let out a groan. I couldn't move, and my voice had disappeared. But my eyes took everything in. I watched my uncle deal with unexpected shock and pain. Then I noticed unpleasant sensations begin surging through my stomach. Intense heat moved up into my chest, through my throat, and settled in my face and under my scalp.

Struggling to recover, Hank slowly picked up the monkey wrench. Then with difficulty he stood up and began climbing up the ladder. I had no plans as to what to do next. My brain was vacant, and my body was burning.

I waited quietly as he climbed to the top rung and stepped out of the well. Hank was not a tall man, but he was imposing in other ways. He usually wore a stern facial expression, and his neck, arms, and hands were thick and muscular. I saw the heavy wrench dangling from his right hand as he walked up to me. As we stared at each other silently, I realized that I didn't really know Uncle Hank very well. I had no idea what he would do. After a few moments, his lips formed three words as he gruffly handed me the wrench:

"Try it again."

HENRY BAADE

HENRY Baade was an aging Oklahoma farmer who tried to pass as a cowboy. He sported a huge white cowboy hat and colorful cowboy boots as part of his daily work attire. With an ample belly hanging over his Wrangler jeans, he drove his pickup truck as if he were riding an untamed bronco. During the wheat harvest, he'd come by Uncle Hank's place from time to time to see how things were going. We could tell he was heading our way by the red dust cloud that followed his pickup as he careened down the road in our direction. Henry's old green truck would emerge from the dust as he raced into the wheat field where we were working. When his truck slid to a stop, he'd hop out, talking loudly and spitting tobacco juice, both at the same time.

Henry had a lot to say but was always in a hurry. So, his visits were brief. Uncle Hank would usually just stand and listen for a few minutes while Henry bellowed and spit. I was never sure if Henry was giving Hank advice, complaining about the weather, or talking politics. Once Henry finished ranting, he'd jump back into his truck, spit tobacco juice out the window, and roar off in a cloud of red dust.

This was my first summer on the farm, so I thought it best to keep my distance from Henry, at least for a while. But after several of Henry's visits, I felt my curiosity growing. So, the next time Henry blew into our field to talk with Hank, I sidled over in their direction and checked out his pickup.

Up close, the truck did not look to be in good shape. It originally was painted green, but the whole driver's side – from the front door to the back fender – was covered in brown rust. However, as I walked around the truck, I was surprised to see not a speck of rust on the passenger side. It was all green from front to back. Circling the truck, I came back to the driver's side and leaned against the rear fender, listening to Henry's relentless barrage of words. Hank, a man of few words, stood close by, quietly listening.

Henry's lecture made no sense to me, but I did figure out something just as revealing. My first clue was the deep pungent odor coming from the driver's side of Henry's truck. I couldn't place the smell exactly, but it was sharp and penetrating. I also noticed that the rust on the side of his truck had an unusual sheen, as if it had been applied in multiple layers with thick viscous strokes.

After a minute or so, I decided to move closer to Uncle Hank and Henry. To my surprise, walking away from the truck was not so easy. The seat of my pants was stuck to the fender. Then, when I pushed against the fender to free my pants, my hands stuck to the surface. That's when I realized the fender was covered with an oozing brown substance. As I struggled to pry myself loose from the truck, my shirt, hands, and pants became smeared with a sticky, smelly, paste.

Whatever was on the fender, it was not rust.

I managed to free myself just as Henry finished his monologue. He was still talking to himself as he walked to the truck, opened the door, and jumped in. As he sped away, I saw Henry lean his head out the window and let fly a mouthful of tobacco juice. Picking up speed, he spit again. The hot wind plastered the brown concoction along the driver's side of his truck.

With years of repetition and plenty of red dust, the hot Oklahoma sun took care of the rest.

TORNADO

I**T WAS** the middle of the night and Uncle Hank was shouting for everybody to wake up. His voice was high pitched and tense. The loud, fierce sound of howling wind penetrated the walls of the farmhouse and the windows shook and rattled, threatening to shatter.

After quickly pulling my younger cousins from their beds we all ran through the kitchen to the back door. The wind pushed against the door so hard that at first it wouldn't open. Uncle Hank put his shoulder against it and gradually forced the door to yield. When it opened, we all headed outside.

It was only about twenty-five feet from the house to the storm cellar, but the trek was slow going. The tornado was so strong that we could not stand up. We had to lie flat on the ground, chest down, and crawl through the grass. Uncle Hank led the way through the darkness, followed by my three cousins, Aunt Arlene, and me. Hank kept turning around to shout instructions at us, but we couldn't hear a word he said because the wind was shrieking so loudly. All we saw was his mouth moving up, down, and sideways as he yelled for us to hurry.

As we all crawled toward the cellar, I glanced to my left and was amazed to see what the wind was doing to Hank's small stand of fruit trees. The trees were bent over at an impossible angle with the top branches scraping against the ground. Several trees had been uprooted and blown away.

The cellar door lay almost flat to the ground. We crawled up to it and Hank used all his strength to yank the door open. His mouth worked furiously, forming words that we knew but could not hear: "Get inside! Now!" We crawled in and climbed down the steps into a small dark chamber. Hank pulled the door shut behind us, locked it tight, and followed us into the darkness.

With the cellar door shut, the howling of the tornado receded into the background and we could finally hear each other speak. Hank lit a lantern so we could see each other and check out our surroundings. There were a couple of chairs and a bench on the dirt floor, and a shelf on the wall held jugs of water, canned food, and a few blankets. We were all safe.

A couple of hours later, Hank climbed up the steps and opened the cellar door. The tornado had moved on, and the early morning sky was brightening. We all felt an eerie sense of anticipation. What would we find? Would the house still be there? Would the barn still be standing? Did the cattle survive?

Fortunately, the damage was minimal. A few trees had blown away, a window was broken, and some random debris had blown from elsewhere onto the yard. The cattle had survived but were milling about. Their water trough had blown away and they were thirsty.

Things did not go as well at the neighbor's farm down the road. They had lost their barn roof – it was later found lying at the far end of their wheat field. The house also suffered serious damage, and they had lost some livestock. Their farm had been in the direct path of the tornado. Thankfully, no one in the family was hurt.

Once Uncle Hank and I finished checking out the surrounding area, we returned home for breakfast. As we walked in the back door, Aunt Arlene and my cousins were busy in the kitchen, big smiles on their faces. It was time to celebrate our good luck.

Breakfast was a full-on feast: scrambled eggs, ham, bacon, sausages, fried potatoes, toast, biscuits, pancakes, cream of wheat, orange juice, and coffee. No one left the table hungry.

LESLIE

AUNT LINDA

INDA was my favorite aunt. Her son, Leslie, was my favorite cousin.

Aunt Linda was my mother's sister and lived with her family on a farm in central Kansas. It was always an exciting time when we went to visit them. As soon as we drove into their driveway, my Aunt Linda would run out of the house to greet us. She was alive with joy and expressed her love with a full and open heart. Her voice would elevate to a higher octave as she showered us with warm and wonderful words of welcome. Aunt Linda's words were backed up by a radiant smile and a huge hug. She was a lovely woman in every way.

During one of our family visits, Leslie told me about a secret gun he discovered in his parent's bedroom closet. He wanted to show me the gun, but we were both only ten years old, and he didn't want his parents to catch us. So, we waited down the hall in Leslie's room until my uncle left the house and went to the barn.

We continued to wait until we heard Aunt Linda go into the bathroom down the hall and turn on the shower. This was our opportunity. We now had a few minutes alone and quickly slipped into my aunt and uncle's bedroom.

Once inside, Leslie opened the closet door and reached up to a high shelf where the gun was hidden. Carefully, he brought the gun down and carried it over to me for closer inspection.

The gun was a twelve-gauge shotgun, big and heavy. We could sense its power by running our hands over the dark wooden stock and the steel barrel. Speaking in hushed tones, we took turns holding the gun to our shoulder and fingering the trigger. All the while, the sound of Linda's shower was coming from the bathroom next door.

We should have noticed when the shower ended. But we were focused on the shotgun. Suddenly the bedroom door opened, and Aunt Linda walked in. She was drying her hair with a towel and looking down, and so didn't see us at first.

What we couldn't help but notice was that Aunt Linda had no clothes on.

Leslie and I just sat there for a moment, stunned and sheepish, holding the forbidden shotgun. But Aunt Linda kept drying her hair, her head down. So, Leslie quickly slipped the shotgun under the bed.

Then Aunt Linda looked up and saw us sitting on the bed staring at her. She calmly wrapped the towel around her body and, with a slight smile on her face, gave us a beautiful scolding.

"You naughty boys! Just waiting to see me after my shower!"

Leslie and I left the bedroom in a hurry. We had been lucky. She hadn't noticed the shotgun.

FINE WINE

IT WAS the late fifties when Leslie began experimenting with mind altering substances. We were both eleven years old and I was visiting him at his family farm in Kansas for a few weeks in the summer. After I arrived, he secretly showed me a recipe for making wine at home. He had found the recipe in an old magazine and was excited to give it a try. We were both raised as Mennonites and prohibited from drinking alcohol. So, we naturally jumped at the chance to make our own.

The first thing we did was to simplify the wine recipe. The fermentation process required multiple steps and took a substantial amount of time. We decided to overlook those steps and just focus on the essentials.

According to Leslie, all we needed was a half-gallon of Welch's Grape Juice and a bottle of grain alcohol. Those two ingredients, along with heat and time, would open the door to our first taste of wine.

Using this simplified format, we filled a glass jug with grape juice, added the grain alcohol, sealed it with a cork, and headed out behind the barn where the sun was hottest. There we dug a shallow hole, dropped in the jug, and covered it with a thin sheet of plywood. We had supplied the ingredients, the sun would provide the heat, and time would take care of itself.

The summer heat was intense over the next few days and time seemed to slow down. Leslie and I were excited about testing our home brew. But we were Mennonites. We were well-disciplined and patient, holding off the urge to dig up the wine jug. The fermentation process proceeded at its natural pace.

Until the fifth day. That's when we succumbed to temptation.

It was the hottest part of the day, mid-afternoon, when we went behind the barn and pulled the plywood off the hole. Our glass jug lay there, holding a thick dark fluid with viscous clumps of green fermented matter suspended throughout. The jug was hot to the touch and the fluid inside was really cooking. Leslie smiled with satisfaction as he slowly twisted the cork. The cork exploded off the top of the jug and a sharp stench immediately assaulted our nostrils. Leslie held the jug high in the air and announced that the wine was fine, ready for drinking.

The first few sips were the harshest. We drank the hot broth directly from the jug. Leslie insisted that the wine would improve if we continued to drink. He emphasized that some personal suffering was required.

And suffer we did. What Leslie and I drank continued to cook in our stomachs. After about five minutes, our bodies began to revolt. Leslie explained that to fully complete our experiment we would need to undergo necessary purging. I was ready to comply. Purging continued for some time.

Once the purging was completed, we lay flat on the hot ground. We baked in the sun as the earth heaved and the clouds whirled dizzily in the sky. A half hour later, Leslie groaned and rolled over to where the jug lay on its side. There were still a few inches of wine left. With another groan, Leslie turned the jug over and poured the last drops of our wretched broth into the fermentation hole.

Years later, whenever Leslie and I went to a party, I noticed that he abstained from red wine. He preferred to drink beer. Cold.

ICE LAKE

W E WERE both about twelve years old and should have known better. Leslie went out on the ice first. I followed. He had that dangerous gleam in his eye, looking for a thrill and not considering the consequences. I was more cautious but was also easily influenced – particularly by Leslie.

The lake was a one-mile walk from Leslie's house. It was extremely cold that day, giving us the impression that the lake's layer of ice must be thick and secure. This was true around the edges of the lake, where we skipped stones, ran, and slid on the ice.

But Leslie soon tired of these activities and was drawn to a more exciting venture. I saw his eyes stray out to the center of the lake and heard him chuckle to himself. Then, sliding one foot ahead of the other, he began moving slowly over the ice, further away from the shoreline and towards the center.

The further out he went, the greater Leslie's anticipation of danger. His carefree attitude was infectious, and I found myself moving in the same direction, away from the shore.

As we moved towards the center, the ice was getting thinner. What had provided a sense of solidity beneath our feet began to feel more buoyant and flexible. Soon we saw hairline cracks shooting through the ice with each sliding footstep. Leslie's chuckle grew louder and was soon a gleeful cackle of delight. He had been captivated by danger.

As we approached the center of the lake, the hairline ice fractures beneath our feet grew larger, groaning and snapping in a frightful way. I finally realized I had gone far enough and decided to turn around. That's when I heard the loud cracking sound of breaking ice and saw Leslie disappear into the freezing water. The ice continued to crack in a zig zag line directly to where I was standing. Then it gave way and I went down too.

When I resurfaced, Leslie was laughing hysterically as he struggled in the icy water. Our heavy coats and boots were no help. After a few minutes of effort, we both managed to get to the edge of the ice break and our feet found the lake bottom. However, whenever we tried to climb out of the water chunks of ice would break off in our hands. So, we continued to break off the ice and slowly make our way back. Closer to the shore the ice was thicker, so we were able to drag ourselves out of the water and onto the ice.

Back on land, the wind and chill tore right through our wet coats and pants. Walking a mile back to

Leslie's house could be a problem. We didn't have a lot of time. Hypothermia would set in soon and slow us down. So, we set off at a run. As Leslie and I ran along, the cold air began to numb my face, hands, and feet. I felt miserable. Leslie was cold too, but our precarious situation had made his day. He laughed all the way home.

MUSTANG RALLY

IT WAS late afternoon under a hot Kansas sun. Leslie and I, now sixteen years old, had been riding John Deere tractors all day, plowing wheat fields since seven in the morning. It was the end of summer and the grueling weeks of plowing were coming to an end. The golden fields of wheat had been harvested earlier in the summer, and the remaining stubble was now plowed under. Dark brown furrows of plowed earth formed graceful patterns across the fields as far as the horizon.

We drove our tractors up to the barn and turned off the engines. We were done. Leslie climbed down first. He never wore a shirt or hat when he worked and was tanned to a dark chestnut brown. With my light skin, I had to wear a shirt in the afternoon when the sun was hot. I also had a small bandage covering the bridge of my nose, which was burned and peeling from too many days in the sun.

Leslie and I stretched our legs and walked over to the outdoor shower. The water tank above the shower had been warming in the sun all day, so the dust and wheat chaff that coated our bodies slid off easily with the help of Aunt Linda's hand-made soap. As we cleaned our bodies, I felt an invigorating sense of renewal. Summer's work had ended, and this evening would be a time of celebration.

We heard the light green Mustang coming from a mile away. It had a 289-cubic-inch V8 engine and came equipped with a four-speed transmission and glasspack mufflers. The Mustang was owned and driven by Buford, a field hand from the neighboring farm. Buford enjoyed shifting through the gears, both when accelerating and decelerating, and announced his approach with the sharp rippling crack of his exhaust pipes.

A billowing cloud of red dust followed him as he shifted down for the turn into our driveway. He slammed on the brakes in front of the barn and jumped out of his car with a whoop and a smile. His boots danced in the dirt as he slapped his blue jeans and pointed to the backseat. Yes, the Mustang was well stocked. He had a case of Coors and a bottle of Jim Beam waiting for us. It was time to rally and Buford was in good form.

Leslie and I had both just gotten our driver's licenses, but we did not own cars. Buford was two years older and had earned enough money as a farm hand to buy a Mustang. It was a good arrangement for everyone. In Kansas wheat country, having a car was essential for active celebration.

Buford jumped behind the wheel, Leslie took shotgun, and I had the backseat to myself. Three beers were open, and in our hands, before we left the driveway. As we swung out onto the dusty road, the Jim Beam bottle started making the rounds too. Buford shouted with glee as he worked through the gears, the glasspacks crackling behind us as we accelerated down the road. The rally was on.

After drinking and driving along empty dirt roads for ten minutes or so, Buford turned onto a smooth asphalt highway. The road ran straight ahead through miles of recently plowed wheat fields. Telephone poles lined both sides of the road.

We were all smiling and laughing as the Mustang roared down the highway. Then suddenly, with a glorious shout, Buford dropped from his seat and down to the floor. He sat squeezed between the seat and the gas pedal. Buford kept his hands firmly on the steering wheel above but could not see the road ahead.

This unexpected maneuver brought a howl of laughter from Leslie. By looking up from the floor, Buford could see through the top of the windshield and navigate by noting the telephone poles zipping by on either side of the road. Buford shouted for some Jim Beam, and Leslie passed the bottle down to him. After taking a swig, Buford pulled himself back up to the seat hooting with delight. Confidence rising, he pounded the dashboard, rolled down his window, and tossed an empty beer can into the ditch. Yes, Buford was in good form. He intended to celebrate, and his mood was infectious.

As the Mustang gained in speed, Buford's eyes darted left and right looking for other opportunities to revel. That's when he got creative.

"Take the wheel!" he yelled. And. without waiting for Leslie to act, Buford began crawling out of the car window. The Mustang was going over eighty miles per hour at the time and the intense wind forced Buford to grip the side view mirror with both hands as he slowly worked his way through the window and onto the hood. Meanwhile, Leslie was leaning across the front seat holding the steering wheel, doing his best to keep the car centered on the road. Buford, with hair whipping wildly and lips and cheeks flapping in the wind, crawled onto the hood and over to the windshield. He pressed his face against the glass and stuck out his tongue at Leslie and me. Buford made a series of grotesque faces; Leslie continued to snort and giggle. Then Buford turned his body forward. He laid out flat on the hood, stomach down, and flapped his arms as he stared at the road ahead.

I'd seen enough. When Buford finally crawled back through the window and took the wheel, I was on the floor of the backseat in a fetal position. I heard Leslie crack open another beer and offer it to Buford. After a few gulps, Buford caught his breath and shouted in triumph.

When we arrived back at the farm, Buford pulled his Mustang up to the barn and Leslie and I stumbled out. We were feeling a little dizzy. Buford stayed in the car, slapping the steering wheel, and revving up the engine. With exhaust pipes crackling, he threw a few cold beers in our direction and sped away in a cloud of red dust. As he shot down the road, we could hear him hollering, "Off to Wichita! Rally on!"

That was the last I saw of Buford. I'd seen enough.

FRESNO

THUGS

I
T ALL started when Fly flipped the bird at a car on Belmont Avenue.

There was no need for that. But there was always the risk of trouble when Fly was around. He was a feisty guy, slightly built but with an attitude. Fly was always trying to prove himself.

I was sixteen in 1964 and had recently moved to Fresno, California from Omaha. I made some new friends, Rodda, Fly, and Eddie, and we were cruising around town in Rodda's 1948 Dodge. The Dodge wasn't fast, but it was cool. It had a funky look and a comfortable ride. It was Friday evening and we were showing off a bit, racing from the stop lights, hooting at other cars, laughing loudly, and trying to pick up girls. It was a typical summer Friday night in Fresno: fiery hot, and lots of time to kill.

Fly soon got bored and began looking for ways to escalate our social interactions. He didn't wait long. At a stop light, we pulled up next to a pimped-out car filled with four or five menacing young men. Their hair was greased back, their shirts were off, and the car radio was thumping out an ominous beat. Our cars waited side by side as they looked us over. Rodda, Eddie and I looked straight ahead, not wishing to engage. We just wanted the light to change so we could move on. But Fly, seeing an opportunity for trouble, rolled down his window and flipped them off. What was he thinking!

When the light turned green, we pulled away and the thugs followed close behind us. Trying to lose them, we turned onto a side street, but they turned too and continued to follow us. The other car was now right on our rear bumper. On the next block they maneuvered around us and blocked our way with their car. Rodda brought the Dodge to a stop and Fly jumped out, hurling profanities at the other car. The rest of us slowly got out of the car and formed a fighting line next to Fly. The situation required a show of strength.

Then the four greasers crawled out of their car. Three were wiry and tall; the fourth was shorter and stocky, a beer belly hanging low over his belt. So far, so good. Rodda was the strongest guy at Roosevelt High – he could bench press over 300 pounds. I was an all-star football player, and Eddie was tough and athletic. Fly was on the small side but carried a bad attitude. We could handle this.

We had miscalculated. The stocky guy went to the trunk, opened it, and began handing out weapons to his buddies. Then, without a word, they advanced in our direction. One was swinging a baseball bat. Another flashed a knife. Next to him, a tall skinny guy swung a long bicycle chain in broad circles over his head. The stocky guy sauntered forward with a pool cue cocked on his shoulder. Seeing them coming at us with weapons, Fly dropped his fists, turned around, and ran. The rest of us looked at each other, saw Fly on the run, and did the same. We were out of there.

Unfortunately, the Dodge was left behind and became the target of choice for the thugs. When we stopped running, we could hear the sound of the baseball bat, bicycle chain, and pool cue taking down the big funky Dodge. Windows were shattered and the hood, fenders, and dashboard were pummeled mercilessly. The knife sliced the seats open and tore through the felt headliner. When the mayhem was complete the thugs drove off into the night.

As we heard the thugs drive away, Fly shouted obscenities in their direction and flipped them the bird once more.

The next weekend, Rodda, Eddie and I were back on Belmont Avenue. This time we cruised in my car. Fly was not invited.

BASQUE COUNTRY

IT WAS late Friday night when the phone rang. Our high school quarterback, Tony, asked if I wanted a weekend job. Tony's uncle had moved to the Fresno area from the Basque region of Spain a few years earlier and was now raising sheep in the hills outside of town. Tony said his uncle needed a player from the football team to help with some heavy lifting. The heavy lifting would involve sheep. Tony also mentioned that his uncle was paying $8 per hour. The typical pay for jobs high school kids got in 1964 was less than $2 per hour. So, I signed on.

Tony picked me up early the next morning and drove us about twenty miles outside of town. We turned off the highway and continued down a curving dirt road deep into the hills. Everything was uniformly covered with dry brown grass. The air was hot and dusty. It was a good place to raise sheep.

Driving around a small hill, we saw a large flock of sheep just ahead. Tony whistled and said there must be at least five hundred of them. It looked like more to me. Two Basque shepherds were moving through the flock separating the lambs from their mothers. Several hundred lambs were herded into a large fenced-in corral. They were bleating for their mothers. The mothers, waiting outside the corral, bleated in return.

Tony pulled his car up and parked next to a small trailer home. We climbed out of the car and into the hot, dry, Central Valley air. Tony's uncle, Sebastian, came out of the trailer with a wave and a smile. He was wearing long heavy overalls over a bare hairy chest. He was built short and wide with a thick neck, muscular forearms, and large gnarly hands. Smiling happily, Sebastian greeted us with a big thump on the back and a few words in Basque. Then he laughed loudly, showing his teeth. They were spectacular. The incisors were sharp, prominent, and protruding. Their coloring was like old ivory, a deep shade of yellow.

Not far from the trailer a long sturdy table stood starkly on the grass. There was only one chair, placed at the near end. On the table lay a sharp knife, a large bucket, and a bottle of whiskey. Sebastian, smiling broadly, took his seat on the chair. The two shepherds had finished separating the lambs and were now standing silently behind the table next to Sebastian. One held a large syringe, and the other a gallon of antiseptic fluid. Sebastian waved his knife in the air and indicated he was ready to start. Tony looked at me and, with a strange smile, said he'd show me what to do.

Tony and I walked to the corral, opened the gate, and chased down a couple of lambs. He picked up one and I picked up the other, both males. It was not easy. The lamb I carried was heavier than it looked. It kicked and wriggled, struggling to escape. But I held it tight against my chest and followed Tony back to Sebastian's table.

Tony held his lamb upright with its back against his chest and spread its back legs wide. He placed it butt-down on the table. The first shepherd was ready and quickly swabbed the lamb's groin with antiseptic. Tony then slid the lamb, butt-down, to the second shepherd who, with the large syringe in hand, brusquely administered an inoculation to the lamb's right hip.

Continuing down the table, Tony slid his lamb, groin exposed, in front of Sebastian. Still smiling, Sebastian grabbed the lamb's scrotum with his thick left hand, picked up the knife with his right, and sliced off the tip of the scrotum. Then, without missing a beat, Sebastian squeezed the scrotum more firmly until the lamb's testicles emerged through the freshly cut opening. Bending over the lamb's groin, Sebastian opened his mouth, dug into the testicles with his sharp yellow incisors, and, yanking his head back, pulled the "oysters" out in one swift motion. The lamb, who had been struggling throughout, gave one agonizing bleat, and then went limp. Sebastian bent over the bucket and spit out the testicles. They looked glossy and soft, like pink egg yolks. Tony put the lamb on the ground and it painfully wobbled off, bleating for its mother. Sebastian took a big slug of whiskey, a satisfied smile on his face.

My lamb was next.

By the end of the day, over a hundred young rams had lost their virility. Only one or two of the larger ones were selected to go free and mature naturally with the flock. Sabastian continued to sit at the table, smiling. He had taken a slug of whiskey after each procedure and his "oyster" bucket was full and overflowing.

Tony and I were invited to join Sabastian for dinner. He and the two shepherds planned to prepare their specialty, "roasted oysters."

I graciously declined.

OFFICER CRANE

A s WE left the Central Valley and ascended the Coast Ranges, I reflected on my mom's last words when I left home that morning. "You're going to get in trouble with these guys," she said. "Stay home!" We were on our way to Santa Cruz in a black Cadillac hearse, courtesy of my high school buddy, Rodda. True, my group of friends did include some questionable characters. But they were serious about celebrating high school graduation and I didn't want to miss out.

As Rodda pulled the hearse up to the beach, there were a lot of eyes checking out our vehicle. It was an early 1950s model and had lost some of its original luster. But the engine ran well, the ride was smooth, and there was ample room to stretch out and relax. Our beverage cooler was also conveniently placed in the casket compartment behind the back seat.

There were five of us, and all but one was a recent graduate. We sat on the hood of the hearse, smoking and taking in the beach scene. A few of us tried out the surf, but it was too cold for more than a brief dip. As the sun began to drop into the ocean, we climbed back in the hearse and drove a few short blocks to our motel.

Our room was on the second floor and had a large outside deck with the required number of lounge chairs. Hanging out on the deck, Rodda dispensed beverages from the cooler as we watched the sun disappear beneath the ocean. The street below was filled with revelers. Some were recent high school graduates like us. But many were college students or local townies enjoying the weekend.

We were boisterous but well behaved, focusing on enjoying some cool brews and taking in the sea breeze. A little later, as the night grew cooler, we pulled on our sweatshirts. Rodda's sweatshirt was bright yellow.

As we talked and drank beer, Rodda noticed someone sprinting down the street below us, heading toward our motel. The sprinter was a young man, tall and lean, with light brown hair. When he reached the motel, he swerved down a side alley and dashed off into the dark. All we could see was the yellow shirt on his back as he disappeared from view.

At the same time several police cars, sirens blaring, were rushing up the street in our direction. The sudden appearance of police activity automatically sent a shiver of fear running through my group of friends. Several of us had been on the wrong side of the law once or twice during our high school years in Fresno. Our reaction was simultaneous: we jumped up from our lounge chairs and ran into the motel room. Rodda, in his bright yellow sweatshirt, was particularly quick on his feet.

Once inside our room, we waited for the cops to drive by and continue down the street. But they didn't. We heard the police cars screech to a stop on the street below. Then we heard several policemen run up the stairway to our deck. That was enough for Rodda. Thinking quickly, he whispered for us to get in bed and pretend to be asleep. Rodda pulled off his yellow sweatshirt and threw it on the floor. We all did the same, throwing our shirts on the floor, and jumping into our beds.

There was a horrific racket as the cops pounded on our door with their night sticks. Angry voices shouted, "We know you're there – we're coming in!" Rodda got out of bed and unlocked the door. Several policemen immediately rushed in, shining their flashlights on each of our faces. When their flashlights landed on my face, one of them shouted, "That's him!" Enraged, they dragged me out of bed, shoved me up against the wall and handcuffed me. The head policeman, Officer Crane, saw Rodda's yellow sweatshirt on the floor and bent to pick it up. "I'm taking your shirt for evidence," he told me. "You'll pay for what you did." As they pushed me through the door and out on the deck, I began to protest. Something had gone seriously wrong here. I was not so much afraid as confused.

When I reached the top of the stairs, Officer Crane shoved me from behind and I began to tumble. With hands cuffed behind my back, it was difficult to catch myself. Luckily, I landed against a railing and came to a stop. I immediately swung around and stepped forward to confront Officer Crane. The first thing I saw was Officer Crane's 45 caliber pistol pointing at my face. "Try something, just try something. I'm ready for you this time." he growled. That was a sobering moment. My protests ended abruptly.

A half hour later, I was in a jail cell, at a loss to understand what had just happened. Whenever I asked for an explanation, the cops would give the same reply: "You know what you did." Being left in a cold cell all night with no shirt and no blanket was not a good sign either. The bed was a thin sheet of steel with small air holes punched through it. The steel was too cold to lie on, so I just paced back and forth in the cell that night.

Rodda came through with bail money the next morning and we headed back to Fresno. The trial was set for the following month. I had been charged with felonious assault on a police officer. Apparently, I bore a striking resemblance to a young man who had attacked Officer Crane in one of the Santa Cruz night clubs. The man then fled down the street toward our motel. He was the young man we had seen the night before, running in our direction and wearing a bright yellow shirt. As the police gave chase, the suspect was able to slip away into a dark alley by the motel. Meanwhile, the police spotted Rodda running from the deck into our motel room. His yellow sweatshirt stood out in the dark.

At the trial, Rodda and several other friends testified on my behalf. I was the last one to take the stand. My lawyer, Rodda's uncle, had prepared me well. I was neatly dressed in a suit and tie and had a fresh haircut. He also suggested that I wear a pair of glasses to appear more studious. Maybe these things helped. What I remember most was seeing Officer Crane glowering at me from the front row of the courtroom. During his own testimony he repeatedly referred to the yellow sweatshirt, holding it up high as evidence for all to see. My mom was there too, sitting silently in the back of the courtroom.

At the end of the trial, and despite Officer Crane's claims, the judge ruled in my favor. I was acquitted.

I smiled with relief as I walked to the back of the courtroom to see my mom. She sat there silently with a stern frown on her face. Then she gave me a scolding:

"You may have fooled the judge, but you can't fool me. I knew you'd get in trouble with these guys, I told you to stay home!"

OCCIDENTAL

BMOC
(BIG MAN ON CAMPUS)

W HEN I arrived at Occidental College in Los Angeles, I brought a lot of Fresno with me.
My first day on campus was in September 1966. It was early morning and I joined the rush of other freshman students walking from our dorms to the classrooms. There was a sense of excitement in the air, but I also felt a bit nervous. Everybody around me seemed cool and comfortable. They were talking to each other as if they were already close friends. I didn't know anybody.

At the same time, I was determined to make a good first impression. I was proud to have stepped away from small town Fresno and was looking forward to embracing a more cosmopolitan college community in Los Angeles. I had high hopes.

To feel more confident, I went with what worked best for me at Roosevelt High School in Fresno. I'd enjoyed some success as a high school athlete, so on this first day of college I sported my high school letter jacket. I looked rather sharp that morning: a nifty crew-cut, wrinkle-free slacks, and shiny new loafers.

A river of freshman students streamed toward the Quad, the central meeting place on campus. Surrounding the Quad were several banks of solid granite steps leading up and out to various academic buildings. My first class was English, located on the right side of the Quad. So, I joined a group of students and headed up the steps in that direction. As the sun shone hazily through the Los Angeles smog, I felt my confidence building.

I was getting the hang of things. I was starting to fit in.

But as I reached the third granite step, my right leg suddenly – and completely – went dead.

It was as if a switch had been turned off. My leg had no feeling, no strength, no sensation, no connection to my body, and no control. My strong, athletic right leg had instantly become a heavy, jelly-like appendage that responded only to gravity.

I immediately lost my balance and collapsed on the steps, stunned. At first, I tried to make sense of things. But as I lay there, looking up from the ground, seeing the shoes and legs of the other students walking by, it all became surreal. A few students stopped to ask if I was OK. Other students thought I must be playing a joke and just laughed as they walked by. I was too confused to respond and just looked up at the hazy sky from my prone position on the stairs.

Feeling the need to act, I rolled over on my side, grabbed the handrail, and tried to stand up. It was no use. My leg was like a dead fish. I lost balance and fell to the ground again. I began to sense a strange new reality surrounding me. There was an oceanic noise in my ears. The trees around the Quad took on weird shapes and began to dance. My voice seemed to stop working too. I could not make a sound. Soon a crowd began to gather. Several students and a professor were leaning over me. They were asking questions and trying to help. All I could do was lie there on the steps staring at their faces. Nothing made any sense.

Then, as quickly as it had gone numb, my leg switched back on. It was suddenly alive again. I flexed my leg and could feel the familiar sensations returning. Within seconds my leg was as strong and athletic as it had always been. I quickly jumped up, and stood upright on the steps, looking around at the crowd of people staring at me.

I could taste the blood on my lip. My letter jacket was smeared with dirt, my slacks were torn, and one of my new loafers had fallen off. I gazed for a moment back at the crowd and turned to head up the steps. I did my best to act as if nothing had happened. I don't think I pulled it off.

BMOC? Not today.

COLLEGE QUAD

PHIL was a particularly annoying individual who lived down the hall from me on the first floor of the freshman dorm at Occidental.

He had a habit of crashing dorm room parties with the intention of quieting things down so he could study. That kind of behavior was understandable during the week, but his unwelcome interventions extended to weekend nights as well. Nobody took Phil seriously, and my group of friends just partied on.

But late in the first semester, things took a nasty turn. Phil reported our party culture to the dorm residence council, and we were put under investigation. A few days later, we were told that all dorm parties had to stop until the end of the semester.

Without dorm parties to keep us occupied, our minds slipped to a more juvenile level of engagement. We wanted pay-back for what Phil had done. After a lengthy discussion, we arrived at a plan which would be carried out at the end of the semester. Our minds were now set at ease.

After final exams wrapped up, we made a big deal of inviting Phil to join us for a celebration. Since the semester was over, and there were no current academic responsibilities, Phil reluctantly agreed to participate.

We were well prepared. Reefers and assorted beverages had been secured. Spirited company was also ensured by having a co-educational event. To make sure that Phil was properly engaged, we assigned a diligent young woman to keep an eye on his drinking glass. Whenever Phil's glass was less than half full, she would top it off. Phil didn't smoke reefer, but several heavy smokers hung out close to him and fortified his breathable air space.

This was Phil's first dorm party and he energized quickly, flying high for a time. However, he could not sustain an elevated state and soon descended into a stupor. As Phil babbled incoherently, we helped him back to his room where he sank into bed and was immediately asleep.

Now was the time to put our plan into action.

As Phil slept, four of us picked up his bed with him in it. Then we carried it down the hall, and out the front door. Our dorm was about a hundred yards from our destination: the Quad – the center of campus activity.

When we arrived, there were a few quiet revelers sitting on the far side of the Quad under a stand of trees. We heard soft guitar music and languid voices singing a well-known folk song. It was a typical late autumn evening in LA, with a warm breeze moving slowly through campus. We set the bed down softly in the center of the Quad.

Returning to Phil's room, we took his nightstand, lamp, desk, and chest of drawers. Everything was carried over to the Quad and arranged around his bed just as it had been in his dorm room. We placed his alarm clock on the nightstand and set it for 9 a.m., the most active time in the Quad. Students, teachers, and administrators would be walking through to start their day. Parents would also be arriving at that time to pick up sons and daughters for semester break. The alarm clock would ensure he was awake for the full experience.

After executing our plan, we went to our separate dorm rooms and slept with a deep sense of satisfaction. At 9 a.m. the next morning we walked to the Quad to bear witness.

The scales of justice were now back in balance.

FIJI HOUSE

JOINING the Fiji House pledge class meant taking on a set of unusual challenges. By meeting these challenges, our pledge class would elevate its standing with the older fraternity brothers. We were committed to making the brothers proud.

One of these challenges was particularly important and took most of our freshman year to plan and execute. The challenge: One of the pledges had to escape from the Fiji House during lunch hour.

The Fiji House lunch routine required that the pledge class wait in the kitchen while the older brothers ate in the dining room. When they were finished eating, the brothers called for the pledges to run out and line up against the dining room wall. The brothers then had the opportunity to hurl random insults and verbal abuse at us. Several bigger and stronger brothers stationed themselves by the exit doors to block the way should any of the pledges try to escape.

This protocol continued through the fall semester, but our pledge class never made an escape attempt. As the months went by, the verbal abuse became more demeaning. By the beginning of the second semester, the pledges were routinely ridiculed as wimps (and worse) because we were too timid to make a rush for the exit doors.

On one occasion, we intentionally made a mock attempt and rushed toward the exit doors, but immediately pulled back and stood obediently in our usual line in the dining room. We suffered increased abuse for the fake escape attempt. But this was all part of our plan.

As the year went on, the number of brothers guarding the exit doors was gradually dwindling. They were convinced we were a bunch of wimps who did not have the guts to make a break for it. But this was just what we wanted.

Their guard was down. It was time to strike.

The next day the pledges arrived in the kitchen early. We removed our clothes and put on jock straps. Then we rubbed grease all over our bodies. Our plan was to line up in a special formation and wait for the brothers to call us into the dining room. The largest pledges would run out first to clear the way. The smaller ones would come next to scatter the defenses. Since I had played football, I was positioned last. My job was to find a hole in the defense, break through, and escape through an exit door.

When the brothers called us to the dining room there was no hesitation. We rushed from the kitchen at full speed, our blockers going first to clear the way. Unfortunately, someone had tipped off the brothers and they were all stacked around the exit doors blocking our way. We were outnumbered and outflanked.

But this was no mock attempt like our first time.

The pledges rushed at the brothers in earnest and mayhem ensued throughout the Fiji House. Greased up pledges in jock straps flew in every direction as the older brothers chased and tried to tackle us. If one pledge slipped through a tackle, another brother would wrestle them to the floor. People crashed against the walls. Chairs and tables were overturned. There was a lot of yelling and swearing as the brothers and pledges grappled. After a few seconds of mayhem, when things were most chaotic, I made my move.

I shot out of the kitchen with greased legs pumping. I aimed for the door with the fewest defending brothers, lowered my shoulders, and put my head down. There was a brief skirmish as the brothers grabbed for my arms and legs, trying to tackle me. But I was well-greased and had momentum. I twisted through the blockade and burst out of the door at a run. I had escaped.

The next day, when our pledge class lined up in the dining room at lunch, the brothers stood up from the dining table and cheered. There was no abuse. We were no longer a class of wimps.

INDIA

ELEPHANT CHASE

RIDING on an elephant feels much like traveling on a ship. There is an ocean of power underneath your body that pitches and rolls, and at the same time moves you steadily forward.

I had just finished my first semester of teaching at Kodaikanal International School in the mountains of South India. For vacation break, I decided to visit Periyar National Park, home to hundreds of elephants – some domesticated and some wild. The primary attraction for me was a visit to the park's elephant camp. That's where I was offered an opportunity to ride one of these remarkable animals.

After climbing up a ladder, I took a seat on top of the elephant's back while the "mahout," the elephant driver, perched on its neck between two large flapping ears. The mahout carried a small cane which he used to guide the elephant, tapping it on the forehead from time to time. After a few taps, and some verbal encouragement by the mahout, our elephant began to lumber off into the jungle. Seated on top, I swayed left and right, rolling with the elephant's long strides.

I was excited at the prospect of seeing other jungle animals from the safety of my seat atop a powerful elephant. I hoped to come across a gaur (the world's largest bison), a wild boar, or perhaps a tiger. As we rode along, the mahout spoke gently to the elephant and tapped it on the forehead from time to time.

After riding into the jungle for half an hour or so, we had not yet seen any sign of wildlife. I was disappointed; it would soon be time to end the ride and return to the camp.

That's when our elephant stopped, raised its trunk, and loudly sniffed in the direction of a thick stand of bamboo. Listening closely, we made out the sound of a large animal moving about deep inside. The mahout, pleased at the prospect of finally showing me some wildlife, directed our elephant to the edge of the thicket.

Suddenly, we heard a loud trumpeting sound and a huge, tusked elephant crashed out of the bamboo. The giant animal's ears flapped as it ran, and its trunk was raised high in the air. Not only did the elephant have massive tusks, but it was much larger than the one on which I sat. The larger elephant appeared to be a male in musth – a time of heavy hormonal activity and a strong inclination to procreate.

Once the mahout saw the bull elephant barging toward us, he immediately began shouting and tapping our elephant on the forehead with the cane. Our elephant responded by wheeling around and sprinting back in the direction of the elephant camp. The large male was in hot pursuit a few yards behind us. Jolting along, I hung on tightly to my seat.

It dawned on me that our elephant might be female.

Sitting on the center of her back, I was not positioned well. That's when the mahout made a critical error. As he frantically tapped on our elephant's forehead, the cane flew out of his hand and landed on the ground. Our elephant immediately stopped running. The big male ran up behind us and prepared to make his move. Not liking my position, I quickly calculated the distance from my seat to the ground, about twelve feet, and prepared to jump. Meanwhile, the mahout shouted and gestured wildly while our elephant stood there calmly and listened.

Then, in a surprising move, our elephant reached down with its trunk, retrieved the cane, and handed it up to the mahout. Before the big male could mount, and before I had a chance to jump, the mahout soundly tapped our elephant's forehead with the cane and off we went, sprinting for camp. This sudden change of pace must have discouraged the male elephant. He gave up the chase and settled on an alternative activity: stripping leaves from a tree and shoving them into his mouth.

When we had retreated a good distance and the male elephant was out of sight, the mahout finally stopped shouting. The rest of the ride back to camp was slow and peaceful. When we arrived, I climbed down from our elephant with a sense of completion. I'd only seen one jungle animal that day. But one was enough.

DHOTI DASH

WHEN traveling during the hot season in South India, I liked to wear a dhoti. Wearing pants was just too uncomfortable for a train or bus trip on the scorching plains. A dhoti is a type of sarong that comes in many styles. The dhoti I wore was the most basic - a length of white cotton cloth that I wrapped around my waist and cinched with a knot at the hip, like you would a towel after a shower. The dhoti allows air to flow freely up, down, and between the legs. The comfort is catching. Even a slight breeze can help make the intense heat more bearable.

The train from Madurai to Chennai involved many local stops. After being lulled to sleep by a rocking train car, and miles of hot dusty landscape, the railway stations provided some welcome excitement. When the train approached, the stations erupted into life. Most inspiring were the many vendors, raising their voices to hawk their goods, *"Coffee!! Chai!! Vada!"* Most travelers stayed in their seats and were served through the open train windows. On this occasion though, I stepped out on the crowded platform to stretch my legs and mingle.

On the platform, I hungrily sampled some blazing hot vada (lentil fritters) with sambar (hot lentil stew) and chutney. The tasty vada were stuffed with hot peppers and I could only finish five of the ten I'd purchased. A hungry dog took care of the rest, gulping them down quickly with a well-practiced technique. The dog hung his tongue out of the side of his mouth as he ate so only his teeth were exposed to the spicy vada.

I followed my snack with a cup of steaming chai. Thinking I had a few more minutes, I wandered to the far end of the platform to buy some bananas at a fruit stand. That was a mistake. As I was bargaining with the fruit vendor, the train whistle blew. A moment later, I heard the chugging of the train engine and the screeching train wheels turning on the tracks. The train was moving out of the station.

I quickly paid the vendor and grabbed the bananas with my right hand. With my left hand, I tightened the dhoti around my waist and pressed the cloth against my hip. I left the fruit stand at a run. Hurtling down the platform and dodging vendors, my dhoti flapped precariously in the breeze. I was soon running along the side of the train as it moved out of the station.

My plan was to find an open door and jump aboard. Unfortunately, the train was filled beyond capacity, and all the doors were crowded with passengers. I was keeping pace with the train but couldn't find an opening to jump on. As I ran, passengers of all ages leaned out of the windows and doors. They waved their hands, and shouted encouragement at me. But the train picked up speed. It was now moving faster than I could run. The very last train car was quickly moving up – the only one left, my last chance.

And that's when my dhoti started to slip.

I had no choice but to use my left hand to grip the dhoti tighter. Unfortunately, I had the bananas in my right hand, and there was no way to pull myself on board. Things were not looking good. Then I saw a young man move aside and make space for me in the last doorway. Two other young men leaned out the door with outstretched arms. The timing was perfect. Holding my dhoti with my left hand, I quickly tossed the bananas to one of the men. Then I extended my right hand and jumped up to the doorstep. The two men grabbed my arm and I was securely on board.

As I walked through the train to my seat, I received all manner of greetings, cheers, and other forms of good will. But mostly there was laughter.

I found my seat, sat down, and tied a secure knot to hold up my dhoti. The air was extremely hot. Then I felt a cooling breeze on my legs. Thankfully, I was not wearing pants. I had my dhoti.

RAT RACE

IT HAD been a hot and dusty day viewing the temples of Khajuraho. The erotic temple sculptures were still fresh in my mind as we watched the sun go down and retired to our rustic hotel close by. I was traveling through India with an older married couple who, like me, were exhausted after a long day exploring the temple site. Their hotel room was a short walk down the corridor from my own.

My bed was reasonably comfortable, and the ceiling fan kept the mosquitos at bay. Relaxing to the hum of the fan and a soft evening breeze, I was soon asleep. Sculpted images of Khajuraho's loving couples followed me into the night.

After an hour or so of sleep, I was awakened by gnawing and scratching sounds coming from the floor next to my bed. The sounds were not pleasant, and I was wide awake in an instant. Sitting up in bed, I grabbed my flashlight from the nightstand and aimed the light toward the sounds. They were coming from behind my suitcase. Then the sounds stopped.

Keeping my flashlight beam steady, I saw a sinister face peek around the side of the suitcase. It was a large brown rat. It had been chewing its way into my bag. I quickly jumped up in bed and clapped my hands to chase it away. It hesitated for a moment and then scurried across the floor, crawling underneath a tall cabinet in the corner.

Seeing the rat run away gave me courage. With flashlight in hand, I quietly stepped from the bed to the floor and tiptoed over to the cabinet.

The cabinet was built from dark rosewood with ornately carved figurines lining its two tall doors. The space beneath the cabinet was about four inches high – the perfect place for a rat to hide. I bent over and shone the flashlight under the cabinet, expecting to see the culprit.

It wasn't there.

I stepped around the back of the cabinet and flashed the beam on the floor. Nothing was revealed. I was perplexed. I had seen the rat run directly under the cabinet. Where could it have gone?

As I stepped back from the cabinet and started turning away, I caught a flashing glimpse of two small red eyes staring at me. But the eyes were not coming from the floor level. They were at my eye level, six feet above the floor.

I swung the flashlight up behind the cabinet and, sure enough, there was the rat stretched and bracing itself between the wall and the back of the cabinet. The rat had quickly and silently climbed up to its perch and was pressing its left front and back legs against the wall, and right front and back legs against the cabinet.

The rat and I stood there silently for a few moments, face to face. Then, realizing it was caught, it dropped to the floor, skittered past me, and raced toward the door.

That's when I noticed the large gap, about three inches, between the bottom of the door and the floor. He slid under and out without breaking stride.

Later that night, back in bed and trying to sleep, I felt a rat run across my chest. When I threw the covers away from me, the rat jumped to the floor and made the same exit, racing under the door and into the corridor. It might have been the same rat, but no matter. I woke up the hotel manager and complained. The manager came to my room and dutifully pointed out the generous space under the door. The cause of my disturbance had now been verified. Solving it was a different matter.

I spent the rest of the night with the older married couple, all three of us in their double bed. I was able to sleep soundly too. Before going to bed, I had checked out the door to their room. It reached all the way to the floor.

WATERMELON

THE watermelon was luscious but not easy to eat. There were too many seeds getting in the way. I had to settle for small intermittent bites of sweet pink fruit while scraping away hundreds of black seeds with a fork.

I'd picked out the melon that afternoon in the Kodaikanal bazaar and brought it home to eat after dinner. It was a good-sized melon and shaped like an egg. One end of the melon was flat and round, the other end was pointed. I ate the pointy half of the melon that evening and left the rounded half on the kitchen counter. My plan was to save and finish it for breakfast along with idli (rice cakes) and sambar.

As I prepared for bed, I began thinking about a rumor I had heard from the watermelon vendor. He had warned me about a Naxalite terrorist insurgency in our area – the mountainous region of South India. Turning off the light, I also tried turning off this thought. But the rumor was alive in my mind, and I took it with me as I fell asleep.

It was about 3 a.m. when the explosion occurred. It was so loud and forceful that I temporarily lost my sense of hearing. My windows were shattered, and doors were blasted off their hinges.

Scrambling out of bed, I was sure that a bomb must have gone off in my home. There was an eerie silence as a thick gray vapor permeated the air. I crept through the darkness and cautiously looked out the window.

No terrorists in sight.

Next, I carefully made my way from the bedroom to the living room. Once there, I could make out several electric wires dangling from the ceiling. They were waving in the mountain breeze that swept through the broken windows.

After a few moments I regained my sense of hearing. That's when I noticed an insidious hissing sound coming from the kitchen. Moving in that direction, I felt water rising from the floor. Soon it was covering my ankles. Thoughts of electrocution entered my mind. Did I dare switch on the lights? I accepted the dare and flipped on the kitchen light. The light revealed a surreal scene, a visual nightmare.

Under the kitchen counter, a broken pipe was gushing water that surged across the floor and into the living room. Lying in the middle of the floor was a shredded hot water heater. The water pressure valve had frozen shut, causing the water heater to explode with tremendous force. The heater had torn away from the wall and was now hissing and sputtering and spewing out steam.

But the real hallucinatory experience came when I looked around the room. The simple white kitchen walls and ceiling were now painted a seductively soft and textured pink. In sharp contrast to the pink color scheme, hundreds of elongated black spots were embedded throughout every square inch of surface space. What had just yesterday been a familiar and comforting white enclosure, was now a garish assault on my senses.

Watermelon juice, pulp, and seeds were plastered everywhere. The rounded half of melon I had left on the counter was nowhere to be seen.

I had a simple breakfast the next morning. Just idli and sambar. No watermelon.

ON THE ROAD

EPISODE 1. It was my first bus ride up the narrow mountain road to Kodaikanal International School in South India. It was a chilly day as buses, trucks (lorries), cars, motorbikes, people, and cows were moving in both directions through tight twists and turns along the two-lane road. On one side of the road there were sheer vertical drops of several hundred feet. The margin of error was not comforting, just a slender shoulder of dirt and gravel before the edge. No guard rails.

I kept my eyes focused on the road. Swinging around the turns, I measured the distance between the bus and oblivion. The bus driver was honking an air horn with his left hand and turning the wheel with his right. Trucks, cars, and other vehicles coming from the other direction honked incessantly as well. Everybody had somewhere important to go. Nobody wanted to slow down.

Coming around a particularly sharp curve, I was surprised – shocked, actually – to see a man lying on the road. Not on the shoulder, but on the black-top road surface in our lane. The bus driver swerved to miss him. Then he drove on as if nothing unusual had happened.

I looked back and saw a truck behind us swerve around the prone man as well. Nobody on our bus seemed to notice. After considering the situation for a moment, I hurried up the aisle and asked the bus driver to stop so we could help the man. The bus driver just smiled and pointed ahead. I looked through the windshield and saw another man lying on the road. His head was directly in line with the oncoming bus tires. The bus swerved again, just missing the man's head. The truck behind us did the same.

I urgently repeated my request that the bus driver stop. He shook his head and laughed. "The men are just sleeping," he said. "The air is cold. The asphalt is warm."

EPISODE 2. A couple of months after arriving at Kodaikanal School, the music teacher, Carl, invited me to join him and his family at a traditional South Indian Karnatak music concert. The concert was to take place at a college several hours away. Carl secured a car and we were soon on our way.

Carl and his wife Margaret sat in the front seat with their five-year-old son. I was in the back seat with their eight-year-old boy. The drive took us down the mountain, across the Tamil Nadu plains, and into a thickly forested region. After driving through the hot dry plains, the forest air was cool and refreshing. We drove through the forest for about half an hour, talking and singing. It was peaceful and quiet. We were all relaxed and enjoying the ride.

Then suddenly we were shaken by a terrible crash and felt a tremendous jolt. The windshield shattered and sent shards of glass flying about the car. Large tree limbs came smashing through the windows, knocking us about and pinning us to our seats.

Stunned, it took a few seconds to realize what had happened. A large tree had just crashed down on the car. The main tree trunk had landed on the hood, broken through the windshield, and hit all of us with its limbs and branches. The pummeling only lasted a second or two and then it was quiet. After a few moments, Margaret began to scream. Carl began to shout unintelligibly. I pushed away a tree limb that had pinned me to my seat and pulled the eight-year-old boy free. Fortunately, he had been knocked safely to the floor. I didn't see any blood. Except for a few scrapes and bruises, the two of us were fine.

Then I leaned forward to check on everyone in the front seat. With all the screaming and shouting it was not clear, at first, whether they were seriously hurt. The five-year-old boy had small cuts on his face, but his eyes were intact. Carl and Margaret had a few cuts and bruises as well, but nothing serious.

We crawled out of the car. Everyone was in shock. Margaret and the boys were crying; Carl was still shouting unintelligibly. I was relieved that we survived.

Looking around, we saw two men standing at the side of the road next to a big tree stump. Each had an axe in his hands. They were tree cutters. Slowly they walked over to us, shaking their heads apologetically. Carl angrily asked why they were cutting trees right next to the road. Their explanation was straightforward: trees that fell on the road made it easy to load the logs onto a truck.

Carl began to shout again. This time he was intelligible.

EPISODE 3. I was riding on a bus late at night on the road from Madurai to Tiruchi. The traffic had thinned out in the evening, which meant fewer trucks, taxis, bullock carts, goats, dogs, and people on the road. The bus driver, with seats and floor space fully occupied, was finally able to make good time. We roared down the straight dirt road with only an occasional honk of the horn. It was late, and with the bus swaying rhythmically, most people were sleeping.

There was a car about fifty feet in front of us and a truck about the same distance behind. Suddenly the car ahead of us slammed on its brakes and swerved sharply to the right. It slid onto the shoulder of the road, righted itself, swung back onto the road, and then without slowing down continued down the road.

A few seconds later, our driver did the same. Slamming on the brakes, he careened sharply off the road and then swerved back on. Several bus passengers were thrown from their seats. Startled, I managed to look out the window to see why we swerved. There it was: a huge yawning hole, as big and deep as a truck, dug into the middle of the road. Road repairs were apparently being made during the day. The workers had left for home in the evening. No signs, no warning light, no safety barrier; just a deep deadly chasm in the road.

Catching my breath, I turned around to look at the truck coming up from behind. Just like our bus, the truck slammed on its brakes, careened off the right side of the road, righted itself, and continued driving down the road. As we drove away, I continued to watch the headlights behind us. Vehicle after vehicle made the same dangerous maneuver. No one fell into the hole. All continued on their way.

EPISODE 4. Another bus ride helped clarify things for me. I was traveling in the evening toward the temple city of Madurai. The bus was speeding along in the middle of a long line of traffic, mostly trucks and other buses. The road was straight, and we were making good time. Looking ahead, I saw that the straight road ended in about two hundred feet. At that point, each vehicle was forced to slow down, make a sharp 45 degree turn to the left, and continue along a different road.

As each truck and bus careened around that turn and sped away, brakes screeched, horns blared, and dust flew through the air.

Our bus came to the corner and began to make its turn. That's when I saw a small cooking fire on the shoulder of the road. It was positioned right on the corner, facing the oncoming traffic. A family of five was sitting around the fire. As the trucks and buses bore down on them and made their abrupt left turn, the family sat calmly, eating dinner.

Our bus turned the corner, missing the fire and the family by just a few yards. No one in the family looked up from their food. They were at peace with the roaring engines, the screeching brakes, and the honking horns. They had staked out their turf. This was dinner time. Life would go on around them.

MANHATTAN

NUMBER ONE
WALL STREET

IRVING Trust had the most coveted address of any financial services company in the world: Number One Wall Street. I was proud to enter through the main door every morning and step into the most beautiful and ornate banking environment in Manhattan. The sculpted walls were inlaid with an intricate pattern of gold and crimson mosaic tiles. Glass chandeliers hung from the vaulted ceiling far above. In the early morning silence, it felt like entering a sacred space, a cathedral.

In keeping with its physical environment, Irving Trust aspired to perfection. All things were done properly and with the utmost decorum.

At the same time, there was a strong human element actively operating just below the surface, and Irving's conformist culture occasionally revealed it's more unfettered underbelly. I began working there in my early thirties. As manager of the Employee Relations Department, I was in a good position to witness this unruly current pushing up from below to soil Irving's polished veneer.

Not long after starting at Irving, my boss let me know about a vexing situation involving one of the bank employees, "Closet Betty." During lunch time, Betty would secretly station herself inside the large coat closet next to the basement cafeteria. If a man opened the closet to deposit his coat, she would surprise him by opening her blouse and pulling up her skirt. Occasionally she would take things further.

This apparently went on for several months before anyone reported it. Once reported, the Employee Relations Department was asked to intervene. Consequently, "Closet Betty" was no longer allowed in the basement coat room. An unforeseen consequence of the intervention was a reported drop in the number of male employees having lunch in the cafeteria.

A few months later, there was a rumor that Betty was now frequenting the coat closet in the more upscale officers' dining room on the top floor. This was either a false rumor or she was too clever to be caught. Whenever I ate in the officers' dining room, I'd check the coat closet. Betty was never there.

The safe deposit vault was the scene for another embarrassing scandal. One of Irving's Vice Presidents would ask his secretary to join him in the vault for a weekly review of his bond portfolio. Once inside the vault, the V.P. and his secretary would enter a private room and lock the door. Their "review" inevitably went well beyond finance. The door was made of clouded glass so they could not see out. However, unbeknownst to them, the clouded glass only worked one-way. Looking in from the outside, the glass was quite transparent.

There were two guards stationed at the vault entrance who monitored all comings and goings. Because of the transparent glass the guards soon became aware of the intimate activities of the V.P. and the secretary. Since they were now witnesses, the guards decided to monitor the situation and gather evidence.

As with "Closet Betty," the clandestine affair in the vault went on for several months. The guards meticulously performed their monitoring activities. However, they were not so diligent when it came to reporting their findings.

One afternoon, the bank President stopped by the vault to check into his own portfolio. The V.P. and his secretary had arrived earlier and taken their private room. As usual, the guards were closely monitoring their activities. When the President walked in, he saw the guards looking intently through the glass door into the private portfolio room.

So, he looked too.

The President was startled by what he saw. Without a word, he turned on his heel, and quickly left the vault. The guards immediately called the Employee Relations Department to make a report: there had been improper use of the vault.

The following day my boss and I met with the V.P. and his secretary. They denied using the vault improperly. So, my boss invited them to join us in the vault.

After arriving, he asked them to stand outside the private room and look through the glass door. Then he asked the two guards to go inside the room and embrace. Upon seeing the guards embrace, I could see the color drain from the V.P.'s face. The secretary refused to look. It was an awkward moment for everyone.

The V.P. and the secretary submitted their resignations. The two guards were transferred to the mail room where their strong monitoring skills were needed.

The efforts of the Employee Relations Department were lauded by senior management. Order and propriety had been restored at Irving Trust.

BICYCLE COMMUTE

WHEN I moved to Manhattan in 1979 my first apartment was located near Columbia University. My morning commute was a 45-minute subway ride from 116th Street and Broadway to Wall Street. The subway ride provided me with some time to catch up on any sleep I might have missed the night before. The train would toss and sway as it rumbled along, luring me into a sleepy, dreamy mind-state. Upon arrival at work, I was well rested and ready for the day.

My commuting routine changed abruptly when the New York subway strike was announced. Now, the city's subway riders had to find an alternative way to get to work. Most people took a bus, or if they were close enough, chose to walk. Fortunately, I had a bicycle. Riding my bike down the westside of Manhattan took less time to get to work than taking a bus. So, each morning, dressed in a suit and tie, I would hop on my bike and peddle alongside the Hudson River until I reached Wall Street. It took me about one hour, not much more time than it had on the subway.

After commuting for a few days on my bike, I became comfortable with the routine and began to enjoy the early morning sounds and sights of the city. I found myself relaxing into a dreamy state of mind, much like I had felt on my earlier subway commute.

One morning I felt particularly dreamy as I peddled along. I had been out late the night before so was a bit sleepier than usual. About half-way down the Westside, I began following closely behind a truck. The truck's back cargo door was wide open, and I could see that it was empty inside. We rolled peacefully along, block after block, one green light after another.

Suddenly, I heard the screeching sound of the truck braking to a stop. My dreamy reverie was broken, and my eyes rapidly focused. The truck had abruptly stopped at a red light that I couldn't see. And since I was following so closely, there wasn't enough time for me to stop.

In a split second, my bike collided with the back of the truck and I flew forward, over the handlebars, and landed in the truck's empty cargo bed. My momentum carried me forward and I tumbled along the floor to the front of the cargo space. Stunned, I lay there for a few moments, checking my legs and arms for injuries. The damage seemed minor, just a bloody knee and bruised shoulder.

Then the traffic light turned green and the truck began to move ahead. I had to get out before the truck gained speed.

As the truck pulled away, I rolled back towards the open cargo door and tumbled out onto the roadway. My bicycle was not far. It lay on the asphalt, just like me. The line of traffic remained at a stop as I slowly climbed back on my bike. Some of the vehicles began to honk. I quickly moved to the shoulder of the road and peddled away.

As the cars, taxis, and trucks passed me by, I saw a lot of smiles. I even heard some laughter. Several taxi drivers gave me the "thumbs up" gesture as well. My knee and shoulder were starting to throb. My suit was torn, and my shirt was smudged and wrinkled.

I was a mess, but when I peddled onto Wall Street, I was mentally ready for work. My dreamy state of mind had vanished.

THE CHAIRMAN

I HAD just taken a new position at the Canadian Imperial Bank of Commerce and my star was rising. Although recently hired, I was promoted quickly and given expanded management responsibilities. I was now in charge of corporate training as well as executive recruitment.

After carefully cultivating my working rapport with other department managers and key senior leaders across the country, I soon felt confident that my elevated status was well-deserved. The bank was profiting by selling innovative financial products and establishing deeper relationships with U.S. corporate customers. My future seemed bright. If the bank was doing well, I should do well too.

Given the success we were enjoying in the U.S., it was only natural that CIBC's Chairman would fly from Toronto and visit us in New York to support our efforts. Once the date for his visit was established, preparations for a reception swung into high gear. In anticipation, I wondered if the Chairman might be curious about developments in corporate training, or whether he knew of any talented executives he would like me to recruit. Maybe he had heard about my promotion to V.P. He wouldn't know my name, but this could be an opportunity to introduce myself.

The Chairman was highly respected and admired both in Canada and in the United States. His career path at CIBC had been rather exceptional, rising through the ranks from an entry level clerk to the pinnacle of authority. He was known to be a proud perfectionist. The Chairman's silver hair was immaculately groomed. His dress shirt, suit, and tie were fresh and crisp; his shoes were polished to a bright luster; and his manners and speech exquisitely refined. The pressure was on for the U.S. to provide a reception equal to his high standards.

A spacious hotel ballroom was the perfect setting for the reception. Crystal chandeliers, lavish draperies, and inspiring views of the Manhattan skyline made for a regal welcome. A variety of fine wines and plenty of champagne stood ready on serving tables by each door. A large selection of hors d'oeuvres was displayed on tables around the room. Cheeses, fruits, pastries, and a seafood raw bar were all waiting to be consumed.

The Chairman was scheduled to speak at 7 p.m. The ballroom was filled well before this. CIBC bankers and administrative executives were chatting, sipping wine, and enjoying the culinary offerings. The level of excitement increased noticeably when the Chairman entered the room. After pausing to survey the reception, he proceeded to move slowly and graciously around the room, meeting and greeting the contingent of U.S. executives. Everyone was on their best behavior. This was the time to make a good impression.

As the Chairman approached the group I was talking with, we all straightened our ties and smiled as we turned to acknowledge him. In a few moments he was in front of me, smiling and offering his hand.

This was my chance. I did my best to appear both casual and confident. Carefully, I shifted a glass of Pinot Noir to my left hand so I could shake his hand with my right. In the same instant, the person standing to my left unexpectedly surged forward to greet the Chairman. His elbow knocked into my left arm, causing it to lurch upward towards the Chairman. There was no stopping the momentum. The Pinot Noir flew from my wine glass. The crimson liquid hurtled forward and onto the Chairman's white shirt and necktie. Some of the wine splattered onto his face and into his eyes.

The Chairman's right hand was still extended toward me, as was mine toward him. Not sure how to react, we silently completed the handshake. As we looked at each other, the Chairman slowly wiped his face with his handkerchief.

No words were exchanged. He didn't ask for my name. And I didn't offer it.

HIGHWOODS

ROAD TEST

THE CHEVY station wagon had been moldering in the garage for over ten years. Originally yellow, it now had blotches of rust and peeling paint on both the exterior and interior. The driver's front door had a broken hinge and hung listlessly to the side. The tires were all cracked and spread out flat on the floor. The car was a lost cause until my brother visited from California. When Jim saw the car, he was enthusiastic about its potential. He intended to fire it up.

It was 1982, and Kathryn and I had just bought a country home in the hamlet of Highwoods, not far from Woodstock, New York. The Chevy came with the estate. The previous owner of the property had abruptly departed town under suspicious circumstances and left many personal possessions behind. We considered these abandoned objects, including the Chevy, to be our bonus for buying the property. Several valuable items had already been reclaimed by us and put to good use. The Chevy would be next.

Jim was a skilled mechanic and immediately got to work. He adjusted the Chevy's carburetor, cleaned the points and plugs, filled the tires, replaced the battery, and made other technical interventions. He lay on the ground, working under the car for most of the day. I could see his bare feet sticking out from under the car as he made adjustments. From time to time, Jim would ask for help and I did my best to assist him. In the late afternoon he gave out a shout. The car was ready.

Jim cranked the starter and the Chevy roared to life. The engine coughed and spat, spewing out black cinders and noxious blue fumes from the exhaust pipe. The muffler was totally shot, so the sound was loud and nasty. Jim just smiled, cranked up the throttle, and announced that the vehicle was road worthy. I wasn't so sure. Jim proposed a road test to prove it.

With our shirts off, and blotches of engine grease on our jeans, hands, and faces, Jim and I jumped into the Chevy, pulled out of the driveway, and accelerated down our country road: Glasco Turnpike. Jim was behind the wheel, long hair and beard whipping in the wind. After easing through each gear in the transmission, he found the floor with his right foot, setting off a raucous roar and leaving plumes of blue smoke trailing behind us.

Jim shouted with delight as he accelerated through the curves, agilely pushing the Chevy through a challenging road test. With shallow hills and abrupt twists, Glasco Turnpike is not an easy road to navigate at speed. But with one hand firmly on the wheel and two feet working the floor peddles, Jim coaxed the car to perform at its best. His smile was ecstatic. An abandoned automobile had been brought back to life and that was a cause for celebration.

Our enjoyment lasted about three minutes. We heard the siren first, and then saw the flashing lights of the police car behind us. Things became complicated after we pulled over. The rust-splotched Chevy had no license plates, no inspection sticker, no registration, no insurance. The blown muffler and toxic exhaust were not helpful, nor was the fact that we did not have our wallets and driver's licenses.

The negative optics extended to our unkempt physical appearance. Within a minute, another police car arrived as back-up. Again, sirens blared, and lights flashed. It wasn't long before a slow line of cars formed on the road. Passing by, drivers and passengers rubbernecked and stared as Jim and I were apprehended.

We were taken to the Woodstock police station, put in a room, and left alone for a while. The interrogation started after they finished their background checks on the Chevy. It turned out that the car was on the "Wanted List" for running illegal drugs from Florida to New York during the 70's. Hearing this, I asked to call my lawyer. It was now clear why the previous owner had disappeared so abruptly. Meanwhile, Jim slipped out the side door of the station and made his way back home on foot. He claimed that the police were making him nervous.

The Chevy was kept at the police station for several days so they could do a thorough search. When nothing was found, the car was released and towed back to our garage in Highwoods. It marinated there for another ten years before I had it towed to a junk yard.

Jim had proved the Chevy could run. Unfortunately, it failed the road test.

COUPE DE VILLE

M Y **CADILLAC** was a vintage 1954 Coupe de Ville with tasteful tail fins, lots of chrome, and bench seats front and back. Six of us piled into the car after an evening of music and cocktails at the Joyous Lake, a night club in Woodstock. It was a short ride to our home in Highwoods and the Cadillac tracked nicely through the curves and dips of Glasco Turnpike. I'll admit to crossing the center line once or twice, but my speed was within reason. I knew the road well.

About a half mile from home, I noticed headlights coming up on us quickly from behind. A car was soon close and within a few feet of my rear bumper. Getting tail-gated on a winding country road can be dangerous and I began to feel annoyed. Fortunately, we were almost home. A few moments later, we crested a hill, turned into our driveway, and drove all the way to our barn. I thought that would be the end of it but, to my surprise, the other car turned and followed us into the driveway and to the barn.

Then red lights began to flash, and I realized we had been followed by the police.

Two officers got out of the car, walked up to the Cadillac, and pointed their flashlights at me. After showing them my driver's license and registration, they asked me to step out of the car for sobriety testing.

The first test was to walk backwards with my hands at my sides. I did a decent job of this and apparently passed the test. But the police weren't satisfied and presented me with a second challenge. I was told to recite the alphabet backwards. This would have been difficult enough in ordinary circumstances, but now I felt additional pressure to perform. The Cadillac windows were rolled down, and my friends were listening. No way I could do this and keep a straight face.

Somehow, I was able to conjure a clear internal image of all the alphabet letters, lined up A through Z. Working backwards from the end of the line, I began to name them without error.

When I finished, the officer asked where I lived. I answered that this was my driveway and my house. Taken aback, the officer said, "Oh. We thought you turned in here to get away." Without another word, he and his partner quickly walked back to their patrol car, turned off the flashing lights, and backed out of our driveway to the road.

After the police drove off, it was quiet again. My friends piled out of the Cadillac and we all stopped to look up at the sky. No more cocktails. No more party. Just a clear night sky filled with stars.

JOURNEYS

LONG'S PEAK

I T WAS late in the day when Chris, Bob and I pulled the station wagon into the campground at the foot of Long's Peak. My friends and I had just finished tenth grade and were on a road trip that included climbing the highest mountain in Colorado.

After setting up our tent and lighting a campfire, we began preparations. First, there was a bottle of Jamaican rum to deal with. That took us most of the evening. Bob, not known to hold his liquor, was eager to enhance his standing with Chris and me. He drank much more than his fair share and soon lost his ability to stand, speak, or remain conscious. Eventually, Bob stumbled from the campfire to the tent. He was done for the night. Chris and I gazed at the stars until the fire went out, and then we joined Bob in the tent. We fell asleep to the sound of Bob retching in his sleeping bag.

Bob was not feeling too well the next morning but was determined to make the mountain trek. He bought a new pair of Converse sneakers for the hike and was eager to try them out. After a quick breakfast of peanut butter and crackers, we each grabbed a small canteen of water, left our campsite, made our way to the trailhead, and began to climb.

The air was cool and clean. We all felt invigorated. Every few hundred yards there was a break in the trees, and a splendid vista would open. Our bodies were young and energetic, so we made good time. Around noon we stopped for lunch (more crackers and peanut butter) and had a brief rest. We sat on a large boulder overlooking an expanse of distant mountains and forested slopes below. Long's Peak loomed not far ahead. This was Colorado at its best.

Starting again, we gained altitude at a rapid pace. By mid-afternoon, we were getting close to the peak. The last few hundred yards were extremely challenging. The summit was over 14,000 feet above sea level and breathing became difficult. Nevertheless, we pushed ahead, and finally arrived at the top. The views were spectacular, and we took some time to relax. We all felt great about our achievement.

It was about 3 p.m. when we started the trek back. Having completed our upward quest, we were less enthusiastic about the hike down. There were too many twists and turns in the trail. Bob was especially eager to find the shortest way back to camp. He had a headache from the night before and was probably dehydrated. And because Bob had not taken time to break in his new sneakers, he was developing blisters on his feet.

So, we decided to leave the trail and take a short-cut.

It was rough going without a trail. With thickets, brush, and loose rocks underfoot, we did not make much headway. There were also many more flying insects. The sun was hot, and we began to sweat. The water in our canteens was getting low and was soon gone.

After a while, the brush thinned out. We made better time clambering across a large open side of the mountain. According to our calculations, the trailhead to camp should be somewhere not far ahead. However, instead of the trailhead, we came to the edge of a cliff. It dropped steeply into a canyon below.

We were getting thirsty and decided to slide down the canyon wall. We hoped to find a stream of water. But when we got down to the bottom, the canyon bed was dry. Redoubling our efforts, we continued hiking, following the canyon bed as it meandered along.

One problem with hiking the canyon was that after a while we could no longer see the sun. We just hiked ahead, letting the canyon take us wherever it would. We soon lost our sense of direction.

After a couple of hours, the canyon came to an end, and we looked out over a vast range of hills, mountains, and forests. There was no sign of a town, campground, or trail. Nothing looked familiar.

We were lost.

Everyone was tired and dehydrated. Taking the way of least resistance, we stumbled though the underbrush and headed down the long sloping mountainside. Bob continued to complain about his blisters. He swore that his sneakers were the wrong size.

Then the sun went down. What had been a warm and sunny day quickly turned cold. As the temperature continued to drop, we began to question the wisdom of dressing so lightly. We were wearing only t-shirts and shorts.

It was now a choice between stopping for the night or pushing on. Either way meant misery. Bob wanted to stop and take off his sneakers, but he was outvoted. Chris and I wanted to keep moving. So, we continued walking into the darkness.

Fortunately, we made the right choice. Within fifteen minutes, we stumbled onto a dirt road. Weary, we sank to the ground and sat on the roadside. There was nothing to do but wait.

Eventually we were picked up by a cheerful group of hikers in a Jeep. They were happy to share their water with us and drove us along the base of the mountain to our camp.

Back at the campground, Chris, Bob, and I were silent as we put on sweaters and lit the campfire. Chris opened a can of pinto beans. Bob limped over to the station wagon. He opened the tailgate, pulled out a canvas bag, and walked slowly back. Opening the bag, he produced a fresh bottle of rum and uncorked it. As the pinto beans simmered, Bob took a long swig of the rum, and passed the bottle.

Then Bob took off his new sneakers, and without a word, tossed them into the fire.

TIJUANA

MY FIRST trip to Tijuana was my last. It was the mid-sixties and a visit to Tijuana was a mandatory rite of passage for guys in their late teens. After driving with a couple of friends to the California/Mexico border, we parked, crossed over, and walked into town.

Tijuana's entertainment district consisted of only a few streets. They were all lined with bars, exotic clubs, and street vendors. Our first stop was at the bar with the most people and the loudest music. The ground floor was wide open to the elements: just a low perimeter wall, a roof, and several well-worn wooden tables. The beer ran freely at twenty-five cents per glass. Rock music was blasting from an overhead speaker. No live Mariachi band here.

After a few beers, my friends and I paid up and walked down the street, stopping at more bars, and enjoying the twenty-five cent specials. In an hour or two we began to feel at home. Everyone seemed friendly and the free-wheeling energy was catching.

Toward the end of the evening we decided to check out one more club before heading back to the border. Our final stop was like the other clubs, but a bit more garish. It was lit up with colored lights and decorated with exotic murals. There was also an enclosed second floor situated above the open-air saloon. At this club, the beers were priced at thirty cents – but they had a Mariachi band. This was a more upscale establishment.

We ordered beers at the bar, drank up, and then ordered seconds for the road. That's when the bartender asked if we wanted to sample some of his special Tequila. Having drunk more than enough beer, we readily agreed. The bartender motioned us to follow him up the stairs behind the bar. There, on the second floor, he showed us a spacious room and opened a large cabinet filled with his tequila collection. The bartender selected his "very best" tequila and poured us each a generous portion.

The room was dimly lit with soft blue lights. Two stuffed couches with low coffee tables were placed against the side wall. Plastic flowers in tall vases were on each table. Around the perimeter of the room were several doors leading to smaller, darkened rooms. There were no windows and it was stifling hot. The bartender poured us a second round of tequila (not his best this time) and went back downstairs to tend the bar.

Then the women came out.

Three scantily clad women appeared from the side rooms and walked over. After offering more tequila, they sat down, one by me and the other two by my friends. They were extremely friendly and moved up close, saying things of a very intimate nature. The tequila and the social interaction were working fast.

As we sat talking with the women, I became increasingly aware of the hot, stale air pervading the room. After downing so many beers, followed by tequila, I began to feel queasy. The room began to spin. I needed fresh air fast.

Standing up, I excused myself and walked across the room and down a hallway to find a window. There was one around the corner at the far end of the hall. I stuck my head out. The fresh air was invigorating, and my head slowly began to clear.

After I felt more stable, I pulled my head in from the window and turned to leave. That's when I noticed two men standing in the hallway blocking my way. One was short, stocky, and smiling. He also held a switchblade. The other, taller and skinny, was holding something in his jacket pocket that pointed in my direction. He gave me a very dark look, cursed under his breath, and demanded my money.

There was only one realistic option here. I opened my wallet and gave the two men the twenty-three dollars I had left. Not satisfied, they told me to take off my boots. This was a smart move on their part. Before crossing the border, I had slipped a $5 bill into the toe of my left boot for safe keeping.

However, their next move was not so smart. Both men searched inside my boots but did not push their fingers all the way to the toe. My $5 bill remained intact.

Dropping my boots to the floor, the robbers swore at me one last time. They then hurried down the hall to the stairs, taking my twenty-three dollars with them. I was not too worried about losing the money. But it was good to see them go.

After pulling on my boots, I walked down the hall and back through the blue lit room. The couches were empty. So were the tequila glasses on the coffee table. The doors around the perimeter of the room were closed. Downstairs, I asked for the bartender. He was nowhere to be found. Nobody remembered seeing my friends either.

With only $5 in my boot, I was no longer a desirable customer. I walked out of the bar and onto the street. I would reconnect with my friends later, but at that moment, I was ready to go home. I headed back across the border alone. The sounds of the Mariachi band slowly faded behind me.

ROUTE 66

M Y FRIEND Jim was behind the wheel of his Oldsmobile 442 as we left Los Angeles and picked up Route 66. It was Christmas break at Occidental College and Jim, his friend Patrick, and I were ready for a change. Route 66 would take us all the way to Jim's home in Oklahoma City. We were excited to be out of school and on the road.

By the time we reached New Mexico, we had learned to keep an eye on the gas gauge. The big Oldsmobile was fast and comfortable, but the gas tank drained rapidly. We drove on, heading higher into the mountainous region west of Albuquerque.

As we advanced into the mountains it began to snow. Then the wind picked up and we soon were driving into a blizzard. It was late in the evening, so visibility was extremely poor. Jim wore thick eyeglasses and was having trouble seeing the road. Fortunately, Patrick and I were attentive and warned Jim when he occasionally drifted off the edge towards a ditch. By focusing so intently on the road, however, we neglected to keep an eye on the gas gauge. When Jim finally glanced at the dashboard, the fuel level had dropped and was close to empty.

We needed to find gas. But mile after mile, there were no stations to be found. Things were getting desperate when we finally spotted a road sign for Lonesome Gulch, a small town just four miles off the highway. Jim was confident there was enough gas to drive the four miles, so we turned off the highway and drove down a narrow winding road toward the town. The blizzard was picking up and the darkness was thickening as we arrived in Lonesome Gulch. The name was appropriate. No one was there. The buildings were all boarded up. It was a ghost town.

Jim turned the car around in the pelting snow, and we headed back toward Route 66. About halfway there, the Olds ran out of gas.

We had two options. One was hiking the two miles to the highway and trying to hitch a ride to Albuquerque. Patrick and I chose that option and began to walk. Jim took the second option and stayed in his car.

Coming from Los Angeles, none of us were prepared for mountain weather. The temperature had dropped into the teens. As Patrick and I walked through the blizzard, the wind whipped right through our thin jackets. We wondered how Jim would stay warm in the car without any heater.

Once we arrived back at Route 66, we waited for a car to come. Unfortunately, there were no cars on the road. The hour was late and road conditions were too dangerous. After a half hour of waiting in the cold, we finally saw a tractor-trailer truck climbing up the hill in our direction. We stuck out our thumbs, but the truck wouldn't stop. We waited another twenty minutes until another truck came roaring up the hill. It didn't stop either.

After that it was just darkness, wind, snow, and cold. No cars, no trucks.

Patrick and I knew we couldn't continue standing out in the cold much longer. We decided to walk back and join Jim in the car. But just as we turned to go, we noticed a pair of car headlights begin to climb up the hill towards us. This time we jumped up and down, yelled, and waved our arms to let the driver know we were desperate. We were overjoyed to see the car slow down and stop.

When the car door opened, Patrick and I ran toward the car, ready to climb in. However, our enthusiasm was quickly curbed. The car was full of men laughing, shouting, and cursing. They were very drunk and there was no room for us to sit.

"Climb in!" The driver yelled. "Join the party!"

Knowing this was our only option, Patrick and I worked our way into the car. Patrick pushed his way into the front seat, and I wiggled my way into the back. It was dark and hard to see, but I could make out two men sitting next to the back-seat windows. So, I inched into the middle and sat down. To my surprise, the seat below me began to squirm and there was an eruption of swear words. I had sat on a sleeping third man. He wasn't happy. I immediately moved off him and crouched down, feet on the floor and head against the roof.

The guy sitting to my right wouldn't have it though.

"Sit down!" he snarled. "You're blocking my view!" I carefully tried to sit down again, but again disturbed the prone body sprawled across the seat below me.

"Get the hell off me!" the sleeping man yelled. I crouched forward again, shifting my weight towards the front. But then the driver got involved and pushed me back with his right arm.

"Just sit on him, he's too drunk to care," the driver growled. This time I lowered my body very slowly. The prone man mumbled a few curses and then began to snore.

As the car drove away, I kept a close eye on the men up front. My friend, Patrick, was wedged into the small space between the seat and the door. The man next to him was bent over, laughing, and trying to locate something on the floor. Then the driver turned to his friends and hissed, "Let's take care of these two guys." With that, he leaned over, opened the glove compartment, and reached in. Patrick and I looked at each other, expecting the driver to pull out a gun, a knife, or some other weapon.

There was no way for us to get out at this point. We were trapped.

When the driver withdrew his hand, there was no weapon. Instead, he was holding a half-filled bottle of whiskey. "This will warm you boys up!" he shouted. The bottle was passed around the car as we sped deeper into the blizzard and into the night.

We arrived in Albuquerque in the early morning. The men in the car had all passed out except for the driver. He pulled into the nearest gas station, wished us luck, and dropped us off.

We paid the station manager to drive us back in his tow truck and look for the stranded Oldsmobile. The blizzard had let up and the sky was clearing, but it was about forty miles to our car. With snow drifts on the road, the going was slow. Eventually we saw the sign for Lonesome Gulch and turned off the highway. Since no one lived in Lonesome Gulch the road had not been plowed. The tow truck slowly carved its way through the white drifts.

About two miles in, we saw a big mound of snow glistening in the sunshine. The Olds was completely buried. We got out of the tow truck, waded through the drifts, and brushed the snow off the car. Looking through the car windows, we saw no sign of Jim. There was just a huge pile of clothes randomly stacked from the floor to the roof. We wondered if Jim had survived.

The car doors were locked, so we banged on the car with our fists. There was no response. But then after a minute or so, the large pile of clothes began to move. Suddenly Jim's face and thick glasses poked through the pile of clothes. When he saw us, Jim grinned and opened the door. He happily told us how he'd taken all the suitcases from the trunk, emptied them inside the car, and crawled deep into the pile to keep from freezing.

The station manager emptied five gallons of gas into our tank. Then, with help from the tow truck, we got the big Olds back to Route 66. After paying the station manager, he drove off toward Albuquerque. Jim, Patrick, and I were all alone again, sitting at the top of the long icy hill.

It was time to move on. We tossed the pile of clothes back into the trunk and Jim crawled behind the wheel. He fired up the engine and headed east on Route 66. The Olds 442 loped along, gulping gas. All three of us kept an eye on the gas gauge the rest of the way to Oklahoma City.

THE MATRON

FTER my junior year in college, I joined a couple of friends for a summer trip to Europe. We bought a used Volkswagen van in Luxembourg and were able to explore most of the Continent during our three-month visit. Operating on a tight budget, we generally ate what we could find in local markets and slept in parks and campgrounds along the way. We did find more luxurious hospitality in England though. But only for one night.

Before arriving in England, the three of us became acquainted with another traveler. Stephen lived with his mother in the countryside outside of London. He graciously invited us to visit him there when we crossed the English Channel later that summer. Given our limited budget, we were quite pleased to hear that the visit would include an overnight stay along with dinner and breakfast.

After spending a hectic day in London, it was pleasant and relaxing to drive through the green, fertile countryside of Kent. We passed by manicured estates nestled behind the trimmed hedges and tidy stone walls that lined the narrow roads. After about an hour, we arrived at our destination. Stephen's home was a spacious stone mansion set back from the road and surrounded by gardens.

Stephen's mother, Mrs. Thornton, embodied the definition of an English matron. She was the perfect hostess: proper manners, civilized accent, and slightly aloof. After showing us to our individual rooms on the second floor, she invited us to join her for dinner in the dining room. My two friends and I were famished and eagerly looked forward to our first home-cooked meal of the summer.

After showers and a change of clothes, we descended an ornate staircase back to the main floor. The dining room was paneled in dark mahogany and the table was set with china, fine silver, and glowing candles. As a maid served the food, we all took turns describing our travels and answering questions. Mrs. Thornton was attentive to our stories.

After the main course, we were served coffee and dessert. The table was then cleared, and the maid sent home. Stephen had an early engagement in London the next morning, so he decided to leave that evening.

Shortly after Stephen said his goodbyes, Mrs. Thornton opened a tall dark wooden cabinet next to the dining table and produced a bottle of single malt scotch. Soon, the tone around the table began to change. Things were warming up, and it was clear that our hostess was more eager to engage than we anticipated. As we sampled the scotch, she began to speak more liberally about her quiet country life and about how much she enjoyed having overnight guests.

After pouring another round, she invited us to join her in the parlor. The parlor was warm and comfortable, with a large curved couch and two stuffed chairs facing a fireplace. My friends and I took our seats on the couch and relaxed in front of the fire. Mrs. Thornton then entered the room carrying a second bottle of scotch, and rather than taking one of the chairs, she curled up on the couch next to us. Grasping our hands, one after the other, she began speaking about the importance of human companionship and the special benefits to be found in intimate relationships. Things soon began to feel awkward. Trying not to be too abrupt, my friends and I gradually excused ourselves and headed upstairs to our rooms.

About twenty minutes later, I was in bed and falling asleep when I heard Mrs. Thornton climb up the steps to our floor. Then I heard her tapping on the door of my friend's room down the hall. I heard his door open and the two of them talking quietly for a few minutes. Then I heard his door close, followed by her footsteps coming closer. She stopped and tapped on the bedroom door next to mine. Again, there was a brief conversation and the door closed. Now her footsteps were coming towards my room. Then came a soft tapping on my door.

I had really enjoyed getting to know Mrs. Thornton and appreciated her hospitality, particularly the home-cooked dinner and the single malt scotch. And she was not unattractive. But as I got up and went to the door, I thought it best to keep it closed. With my ear against the door, I listened as she asked to come in and sleep with me. I began to feel uneasy. She was a wonderful, gracious, and intelligent hostess and I did not want to hurt her feelings. But I was just not ready for this.

Mrs. Thornton continued to tap. She called out to me by name and pleaded for me to open the door. I had to respond in some way. The best I could do was to stand on the other side of the door and tell her I was celibate and studying for the priesthood. I went further by telling her how much I was tempted to invite her in, but unfortunately, my conscience wouldn't allow it. That's when she stopped tapping on the door and slowly walked away, down the stairway, and back to the main floor.

The next morning before leaving, we had the best of all English meals: a hearty breakfast of poached eggs, scones with jam, a rasher of bacon, roasted tomatoes, and coffee. Throughout the meal, Mrs. Thornton once again embodied the definition of a respectable English matron. She was the perfect hostess: proper manners, civilized accent, and slightly aloof.

TANGIERS

OUR FERRY arrived in Tangiers around midnight. Even at that late hour, the Moroccan city was bustling like it was midday.

After checking into our hotel, my friends and I immediately went out to explore the bazaar. The shops were all open and active, and we were energized by our lively surroundings. Carpets, pottery, leather goods, clothing, jewelry, and other merchandise were all on display in the open air. Prices varied widely and quickly dropped if we were willing to haggle.

But candidly, we were really focused on finding just one item: hashish.

My friends and I had joined up with two adventuresome travelers a few days earlier in Granada, Spain. It was their idea that we take a ferry to Tangiers, buy several kilos of hashish, and then smuggle the contraband back to Spain. Once in the bazaar, it didn't take long for us to make a connection.

Our connection appeared in the form of a streetwise boy named Ali. We had only made a couple of inquiries with shopkeepers when Ali cheerfully appeared. With a radiant smile and an angelic face, he immediately knew what we wanted. Ali looked to be about thirteen years old, was fluent in English, and quickly charmed us with his lilting voice and easy laugh. He also promised to produce the highest quality hashish in the city. Without delay, he motioned us to follow him. We could not resist.

We followed Ali to the edge of the bazaar and then plunged into a warren of dark narrow streets. The deeper in we went, the narrower the streets. Soon we were in a tight labyrinth of alleyways. Eventually, the alleys became so narrow we had to walk single file. High walls and upper balconies leaned over our heads. There were doorways every few feet leading to unknown rooms, courtyards, and gardens.

The noise and bustle of the bazaar was far behind us now. The night had turned eerily silent. Finally, Ali stopped in front of a small green door and began fiddling with the latch. The door was locked. Ali glanced up and down the dark alley. He had apparently forgotten the key. Then, with an innocent giggle, he took a screwdriver from his pocket and forced the lock open. Ali quickly motioned us inside, bolted the door behind him, and lit a candle.

The room was right out of the *Arabian Nights*. It was spacious and welcoming, with heavy carpets and draperies, carved rosewood furniture, silk pillows and cushions, brass lamps, and silver candle holders. Ornate brass hookahs were placed conveniently around the room to emphasize the purpose of our visit.

After inviting us to sit down on cushions and relax, Ali went to an ancient wooden chest in the corner. He swung open the top and took out several large rectangular bricks of dark green hashish. Smiling broadly, he passed the hashish around so we could feel the texture and smell the rich resins embedded in each brick. Then he broke off several smaller lumps of hashish, put them in a hookah pipe, and invited us to sample his wares. Within a few minutes, hashish smoke filled the room. The hash was potent. After a couple of refills, we all kicked back and sank more deeply into our comfortable cushions.

That's when the trouble began.

Our blissful reverie was rudely interrupted by a loud banging on the door, and enraged shouts. Before we could react, the door was kicked open and three men burst into the room waiving knives.

With angry eyes darting around the room they spotted Ali reclining in the corner. The yelling intensified as they moved in his direction. Ali raised his arms in the air and loudly proclaimed his innocence. Meanwhile, the rest of us were undergoing a jarring transformation. What had been a serene and dreamy reverie had abruptly become visceral panic. Fortunately, the door stood open. My friends and I exited at a full run. With adrenalin gushing, we sprinted down the alley and away.

We had no clue how to find our way to the bazaar. But getting back turned out to be easier than expected. Whenever we came to a crossing lane, we opted for the wider opening. Keeping to this strategy, the narrow alleys gradually gave way to wider streets and eventually we found ourselves back in the bazaar. By then the merchants had called it a day and the shops were closed. We slowed to a walk and followed the last few quiet streets to our hotel.

The next day was brilliantly sunny. About midmorning we slowly woke up to the bustling sounds of the bazaar. I sleepily walked to the balcony and surveyed the street scene below. In less than a minute, I heard the distinct sound of a young boy's voice drifting through the cacophony of sounds. I looked more closely and spotted Ali calling up to me from the street below, waving and smiling. He had somehow found our hotel and had been waiting for us to wake up.

"Come with me!" he shouted, "I have the key this time!"

Two days later, we all left Tangiers by ferry and headed back to Spain. This was during the time of Franco's dictatorship, and when we arrived at our port, there were military police stationed everywhere. It was not the place to cause any trouble.

I kept a sharp eye on our two fellow travelers as they went through customs. Fortunately, none of the customs officials did the same. A closer inspection would have revealed that each traveler had a distinct rectangular bulge below the belt of his pants.

YUGOSLAVIA

THE FIRST step was to find the American Embassy and report the theft. It was 1969 and Yugoslavia's quarreling ethnic groups were tenuously held together by their communist dictator, Tito. I was in the capital city, Belgrade, without a passport. It had been stolen and I needed a new one to leave the country.

Due to cold political relations between the United States and Eastern European communist regimes, the American Embassy told me they had no jurisdiction regarding stolen property. I would have to take my case to the state police.

My initial attempts at this task were not encouraging. I went from one police department to another with no success. Each police clerk would just stare at me blankly as I told them that my passport was stolen. No one spoke English and I didn't speak Serbian.

It didn't help that I had long hair and a beard.

As the days went by, my traveling buddies were getting restless. Hanging out in Belgrade was getting old. We began talking about taking our chances at the border with Austria where, if I got through, there would be a more receptive government to deal with. We decided to give it one more day and then head for the Austrian border.

That afternoon, I found a police clerk who seemed to understand my situation. He nodded his head and smiled when I spoke. Although he didn't respond verbally, he gave me a hastily written address on a small piece of paper. I took this as a good sign.

The hand-scribbled address I was given brought me across town to an imposing government building on the top of a prominent hill. The structure was built from large blocks of dark granite and had an ominous absence of windows. Access from the street to the building was through a massive iron gate and up a long series of broad granite steps. The steps led to a spacious outdoor promenade surrounded by tall heavy pillars. There was no one in sight.

After walking up the steps and onto the promenade, I saw the first human beings in the area. Two military guards were posted on either side of large iron entry doors. The guards looked straight ahead and held their machine guns at the ready. I quietly walked up to them and managed to get a few words out, trying to explain why I was there. They continued to look straight ahead. They had no idea what I was saying. Although I didn't think it was a good idea to open the large doors by myself, I did it anyway. To my relief, the guards just ignored me.

Even though it was summer, I felt an uncomfortable chill as I walked into the building. Inside was an immense open hall, silent and empty. At the other end of the hall were two large doors. Both had been cast in bronze and featured embossed images idealizing the country's industrial strength. After briefly hesitating, I walked across the hall and pushed through the doors.

In front of me was a long, cavernous, windowless room. A strip of red carpet ran straight from where I stood, through two long rows of massive pillars. It ended at the far end of the room. There, on a raised granite platform, was a huge marble desk. Yugoslav and Soviet flags hung limply on either side of the platform. Next to each flag stood a military guard in uniform. Like the guards posted outside, the two soldiers held machine guns across their chests.

More ominous than the guards was the military officer seated behind the marble desk. From where I stood, I noted his lavishly decorated uniform. Stars, medals, and assorted ribbons spilled over his shoulders and down his chest. He was looking straight ahead, down the red carpet in my direction.

The room was totally silent.

Mustering a degree of confidence, I strode down the red carpet toward the officer. Coming closer, my confidence began to waver. Surges of anxiety roiled my stomach. The officer never moved. He just looked straight ahead, his stone-cold eyes staring at me and through me. His steel gray hair was cropped short. His face, neck, and shoulders were thick and powerful. The military officer's facial expression was not encouraging.

It was one of contempt. My long wavy hair and kinky beard were not making a good impression with this man.

After crossing the room, I stopped below the elevated desk, looked up at the officer, and blurted out the story of my stolen passport. He continued to coldly stare at me. Then his cheeks and neck began to turn red. I was going to continue talking, but then thought better of it. Clearly, he didn't understand me. And he did not appear to be a patient man.

I glanced at the military guards, hoping that one of them might have grasped the meaning of my story. They continued looking straight ahead, machine guns in hand. That's when I turned to leave. I didn't belong there.

It was a long silent march back down the red carpet. I felt their unmoving eyes on the back of my head all the way to the exit doors. Breathing was difficult. I felt better only after leaving the building and walking past the two silent guards outside the entrance. They hadn't moved either.

I walked down the steps toward the street and slowly regained my equanimity. It was unclear what I should do next. Then, at the bottom of the steps, I noticed a well-dressed young man standing at the gate. He was holding it open for me. To my surprise, the young man addressed me by my name in slightly accented English. He told me he was there to help and asked me to come with him. I didn't hesitate.

We walked only a few blocks before turning onto a quiet boulevard with elegant homes and walled gardens. After passing by a few residences, my young guide stopped at one of the entrances and led me to the front door of a large house. Once there, he knocked on the door quietly. Then he turned and walked away.

I was left standing in front of the door, not knowing what to expect. In a few moments, the door opened. An older man stood just inside the entrance. He greeted me warmly and invited me in. We walked into a comfortable living room where he offered me a seat on the sofa. Using perfect English, he asked if I wanted a Coke.

While I drank the Coke, the man told me about his travels and the years he had spent going to school in America. He mentioned that he had met several young travelers in my situation over the last few years and was impressed that I had decided to travel in his home country. When I finished my Coke, he stood up and walked me toward the door.

"I fear you have found our country to be difficult," he smiled. "Unfortunately, in Europe we are still a backward nation. But I believe we will find our way forward."

At the door he said goodbye and handed me a large manilla envelope. He watched while I slowly opened it. Waiting inside was a brand-new American passport.

TEL AVIV

HIJACKING airplanes was the activity of choice among terrorists in the early 1970s. Israeli flights were particularly at risk and several recent hijackings had occurred out of Tel Aviv. My flight was scheduled to land there for a brief layover on my first trip to India, and I was worried.

When we landed in Tel Aviv, I looked out the window and saw Israeli soldiers with machine guns quickly surround the plane. At the same time, the pilot announced that all passengers must immediately leave and go to the airline terminal. I was sitting in the back of the plane so had to wait for passengers in the front to leave first. While waiting, I decided to stand up and stretch. I also wanted to freshen up a bit, so I left my seat and stepped into the lavatory. I washed up, brushed my teeth, and combed my hair. Meantime, everyone else managed to leave the plane. Suddenly things were eerily quiet.

I was almost ready to leave the lavatory when I heard shouts, doors slamming, and other loud noises coming from the front of the plane. A few moments later, there were sharp voices and clanking sounds coming down the aisle in my direction. The loud sounds stopped just outside the bathroom door.

It was quiet for a few seconds. Then the door latch began to jiggle.

The door was locked, but that didn't deter the intruder. Shouting began again, followed by violent pounding on the door. A moment later, someone slammed their body against the door and began to push against it. It was getting scary, but I was determined to hold my own. The door was now bulging inward, and I wasn't sure if the lock would hold. With my back wedged against the sink, I quickly raised my legs, put my feet on the middle of the door, and pushed back with all my strength.

At the same time, I was getting mentally prepared to run if the door gave in. The attacker made several more attempts to break down the door, all of which I successfully resisted. Then it became quiet again. I relaxed my legs and stood up.

Then things got worse.

I noticed a big shiny gun barrel slide through the crack at the bottom of the door. Using it as a crowbar, the attacker began to force the door open. Pushing against the door with my feet would no longer protect me, so I grabbed the doorknob with both hands and hung on. It was useless. The intruder was determined and methodical. As my heart rate accelerated, I put my head down and prepared to launch myself past the attacker and run off the plane.

When the bathroom door popped open, I was ready to charge. But I stopped short. Things were not as I expected.

In front of me stood a short, stocky cleaning woman holding the shiny shaft of a vacuum cleaner. She had used this to pry the door open. The woman was shocked to see me jump out from the bathroom and let out a piercing scream.

Her scream brought more cleaning ladies running down the aisle from the front of the plane. Shouting and waving their vacuum cleaner shafts, they had me surrounded in a few seconds. Then their supervisor arrived and brusquely escorted me off the plane.

Once in the airport waiting area, I stopped and looked around. All was clear.

No terrorists. No cleaning ladies.

CAPE TOWN

THE CRUISE ship I sailed on from India pulled into the Cape Town harbor as the sun was setting behind the mountains. I had been at sea for weeks since leaving Bombay, and the sight of Cape Town's cityscape and mountainous backdrop were a welcome sight. Most of the passengers were crowded on deck to take it all in. Everyone was excited to disembark and find out what the city had to offer. My own explorations would be limited though. It was 1975, and South Africa was held in the grip of apartheid.

During my time on the ship, I had become friendly with an elderly Indian couple who were returning to their home in Cape Town after visiting relatives in India. They had been kind enough to invite me to their home for dinner and I readily accepted. Cuisine on the ship was quite good, but after a month on board, the menu had become repetitive. I was looking forward to a South African home-cooked Indian meal.

The elderly couple's son, James, was waiting for us at the dock, ready to drive us to their home. They lived on the far side of the city and the drive would take about thirty minutes. As we drove along, the sun went down. We were all relaxed and enjoying being together. The couple told James about their experiences in India and about how they had met me on the cruise. They were happy to be back home and on dry land again.

Twenty minutes into our drive we heard the sirens. It was not just one police car. There were several cars converging on us from different directions. James pulled to a stop and we were quickly surrounded by patrol cars with flashing red lights. Our relaxed conversation ended abruptly. We all sat quietly in the car, waiting.

After a few minutes, several uniformed police officers surrounded the car and pointed their flashlights at each face inside. The police took turns walking around the car, shining their lights at us from every angle. So far, no words had been exchanged. Finally, the ranking officer walked up to the driver's door and knocked loudly on the window with his night stick. James rolled down the window.

"Where the hell are you going!" the officer demanded.

"Driving to our house," James replied.

"What's the white guy doing here!"

"My parents met him on the cruise ship. He's coming to our house for dinner."

Then the officer turned to me.

"You can't be with colored people in this section of town. Get out of the car. You're coming with us."

With that, the officer opened the back door and escorted me to his patrol car. I had no time to say goodbye. As we pulled away, the other patrol cars turned around and left as well. I tried waving to my friends out the window, but I'm not sure if they saw me. The forced separation was abrupt and callous. Sheer cruelty.

The officer drove me back to the "white" section of Cape Town and dropped me off in the tourist area. As I walked through the brightly lit streets, packed with restaurants and clubs for white people only, everything felt empty. The surroundings were just a façade, lifeless and stale. I was lonely beyond words.

THE DUCHESS

FTER six weeks on an ocean liner, I was coming to the end of my cruise from India to Europe. Our ship stopped at several intriguing African ports along the way, and those experiences had been memorable. But the many hours spent on board while plowing through the ocean were tedious. We did have one fascinating encounter with a school of dolphins and had spotted a Russian submarine surfacing close by. But the journey had mostly been a relentless diet of hot sun, blue skies, and endless water. Fortunately, the seas were friendly throughout the journey, and we finally entered the calm waters of the Mediterranean.

The bright moments on board tended to revolve around the dining room. The ship's passengers came to dinner dressed in their best, looking to make a good impression. Most of them were German tourists who were completing a cruise to India and Africa. Given the difference in language, my interactions with other passengers was rather limited. At the same time, I came to enjoy observing the various social dynamics that occurred during our meals.

The passengers dining at the table next to me were of particular interest. A stern, stout, bejeweled woman held court over four or five other passengers at each meal. She was dressed in ponderous regal attire and followed an antiquated etiquette that involved much fluttering of an embroidered hanky while keeping her nose pointed toward the ceiling.

The "duchess" as she was known, sniffed the air repeatedly as if testing and evaluating the quality of her surroundings. As she held court at the table, waiters would swarm around her and attend to her needs. Occasionally she would feel neglected, and the wait staff would get a harsh dressing down. The staff would then redouble their efforts to please her. Other than the few people at her table and the wait staff, I never saw the duchess speak with any other passengers.

On the last day of our cruise, about two hundred miles from Genoa, a terrific wind swept off the plains of southern France and roiled the Mediterranean waters. The morning sky turned dark, the wind howled, and the ship tossed about on towering waves. The slow, peaceful rocking motion we were accustomed to became a more ominous pitch and roll. As the morning hours went by, the waves grew larger and the ship rolled more steeply.

At noon, the usual lunch crowd was not in the dining room. Other than me, only two or three passengers felt well enough to eat. Most of the crew and wait staff were not eating either. Everyone was suffering to some degree from sea sickness. I tried to eat but had no appetite and left my table. That afternoon was miserable. Everyone was holed up in their cabins.

At dinner time, I felt a slight twinge of hunger and decided to try eating again. When I entered the dining room, there were a few other people sitting at their tables and a small number of waiters staggering back and forth between the dining room and kitchen. As the ship rolled from side to side, the waiters did their best to deliver plates of food without losing their footing. Given the extreme weather conditions, I was surprised to see the duchess at her usual table, sternly holding court with her attendants.

During dinner, the storm began to escalate. The ship's heavy pitch and roll had been somewhat rhythmic throughout the day, but the waves were becoming more erratic and intense. The pitches became deeper, and rolls became steeper. I noticed the waiters glancing nervously at each other. Their faces seemed to turn whiter with each lurching pitch. I also noticed that my stomach churned, not so much from nausea, but from a deepening fear.

The ship swung from side to side several times, and then began to climb. The far end of the dining room floor slowly edged higher and higher. When the far wall became the ceiling, the room began to rotate. The floor angle was now so steep that the waiters lost their footing and slid down to the low end of the dining room. There was a sense of impending doom. We were climbing a giant wave. It was time to panic.

At this very moment, the duchess gave us an unexpected gift, a gift to help relieve the grip of fear that held all of us in the dining room. As the giant wave peaked, and just before the ship would surely capsize, her table tilted to an impossible angle. All the glasses, plates, and platters of food suddenly slid down the table towards the duchess.

The dishes of food emptied into her lap, and her chair toppled over backward. In an instant the duchess was lying on her back. Her feet were kicking up in the air as she slid down the steeply angled floor. Her stout legs, adorned with pink satin bloomers, pumped furiously while she skidded toward the low end of the room. The duchess made short squealing sounds as she picked up speed. A flailing pile of wait staff was at the bottom, waiting to greet her. When she slid into the pile, things turned chaotic.

Miraculously, the ship had reached the peak of the wave without capsizing. It paused there for a moment and then plunged down in the opposite direction. The duchess, surrounded by a squirming pile of waiters, dishes, and food, began sliding back toward the other end of the dining room. As the pile of humanity and debris picked up speed, I heard a waiter begin to laugh. Another one joined him. Then another. Soon everyone was laughing.

The gift of laughter was contagious. But the duchess did not join in. She just continued to squeal. As the duchess careened down the floor, feet and bloomers kicking upward, she kept her nose pointed high in the air.

ABOUT THE AUTHOR

J OSEPH Schmidt was raised in a Midwestern Mennonite family. He attended Occidental College in Los Angeles during  the late 1960s and then accepted a three-year teaching assignment in India.

After returning to the United States, Joseph earned an MA in Psychology from Columbia University, opened a psychotherapy practice in San Francisco, and worked as a corporate executive in New York for twenty years.

Following his corporate career, Joseph co-founded the New York Insight Meditation Center and served as its Executive Director. He is currently working as a hospital chaplain after training with the New York Zen Center for Contemplative Care.

Joseph Schmidt lives in Ridgewood, New Jersey with his wife, Kathryn. They have two sons and three grandchildren.